SMART MOVES

How to Save Time and Money
While Transitioning Your Home and Life

D1466713

SMART MOVES

How to Save Time and Money
While Transitioning Your Home and Life

CAROLINE CARTER

Library of Congress Control Number: 2019902310
ISBN: 978-1-7336961-1-1 (paperback)
ISBN: 978-1-7336961-0-4 (ebook)

Cover & interior designed and formatted by:

www.emtippettsbookdesigns.com

To Buddy Carter with a lifetime of love and gratitude

Table of Contents

Foreword
By Laura Cox Kaplan

I'm sentimental and a "saver" (some might say "borderline hoarder"). I'm also private -- especially where my personal space is concerned. The notion of having strangers traipse around my house and look in my closets and bathrooms goes well beyond discomfort and sends me into a panic. So, moving for me is a nightmare.

I first met Caroline Carter when my husband and I decided to sell our first home -- the home we bought when we first married, and the home where we were living when both our children were born. At the time, I was working as a partner and executive at a large accounting and consulting firm. I had a demanding schedule and was often traveling. My husband had just started at a tech company and was spending much of his time traveling back and forth across the country.

When we found the house we planned to buy, our Realtor told us we would need to have our current house ready and on the market within three weeks. *Three weeks?!* We both had jobs, two small children, no idea of how to tackle the mechanics of the move or the selling of our house. While lovely, our home had some deferred maintenance. And, while most people have some 300,000 items (as Caroline discusses in the book) that must be sorted and packed or discarded during a move, we had quite a bit more. As an only child and the only granddaughter on both sides of my family, I had inherited practically every piece of cherished china and crystal for generations. While not particularly valuable, this extensive collection could stock the home section of a large department store (or two). My husband and I had also worked for many years in politics and had more than our fair share of assorted memorabilia.

So, there was a lot of stuff -- much of it highly fragile and delicate. We also had a number of home projects that needed to be evaluated to determine whether addressing them was worth it or not. The list of "to do's" in my head was already pages and pages long and we hadn't even started yet.

Totally overwhelmed, I excused myself from the meeting with our Realtors and retreated upstairs to my bathroom. I sat down and tears started to flow as I thought about how impossible a three-week deadline would be. There simply were not enough hours in a day to accomplish all that had to be done in that short period of time.

A few minutes later my husband came to find me. With him was Caroline Carter. I remember so clearly Caroline handing me a tissue while taking my hand and telling me in her warm, no-nonsense way, "You can do this, and I will be with you every step of the way. You just need a plan."

You see, Caroline combines the best of what an experienced professional, and thoughtful, action-oriented therapist would do. She acknowledges your emotional state, but immediately sets about to address it with a plan of action. Caroline did just what she said: Stuck with me every step and helped us create the plan that made our first home transition, as well as three more that followed soon thereafter, seamless (or as seamless as any move can ever be). Most importantly, Caroline allowed us to maximize our time by not wasting it on improvements that were not value added or that wouldn't help us get a higher return. She also enabled me to focus on my own "highest and best use" -- those areas where my attention, or my husband's, was most needed, rather than on every single detail or on things that frankly could be handled as well or better by Caroline or a member of her team.

In this book, Caroline is giving you what she gave me. She has taken the guesswork out of home transition and has created a practical, no-nonsense, how-to plan that every person who decides to move, sell, downsize, upsize or who is relocating for a remodel needs to understand before they start the process. Her advice will not only save you countless headaches but will save you money and more importantly time.

Moving is stressful and one of the hardest things you will tackle -- even under the best of circumstances. I am forever grateful that I had Caroline by my side to walk me through the home transition process. Her practical wisdom and step-by-step approach eased the stress -- emotional, financial and physical -- and helped my husband and me resettle our family seamlessly and efficiently. With her terrific book in your hands, I wish the same for you!

Laura Cox Kaplan is the creator and host of She Said/She Said podcast and an adjunct professor at American University in Washington, D.C. She is a former senior-level government official and an executive at PricewaterhouseCoopers (PwC). She is also a former client.

Introduction

Breaking up is hard to do. No one knows that better than my former client - let's call her Anne - who has left many addresses in her rear-view mirror. At age 52, she has moved three times in the last ten years or approximately every 3.3 years. There was her first transition from Richmond, Virginia to Washington, D.C. for work, followed by a second transition thanks to a divorce where he kept the house, and she rented a townhouse a few blocks away. Add a dash of downsizing during the recession, and a third transition was required to a smaller, but tasteful condo nearby.

If you pull out a roll of packing tape, Anne just might have a physical reaction.

"Even the idea of a cardboard box or those white packing peanuts is enough to send me into a panic attack," she says. "I can't even think about moving without breaking out into hives."

Anne is not alone in her dread over home transition, the process of selling your house and moving to the next home. Chances are, you've already experienced a home transition without understanding exactly which steps you took and their impact on your life. Like most people, you probably survived the process on autopilot, just happy to be done with it. You're not the first, and you won't be the last. According to the U.S. Census Bureau, Americans move more than people in any other country with the average person logging 11 residences throughout the average life span.

Transitioning a principal residence is an emotional, financial, and physical challenge. While the journey is different for everyone, the home transition process is the same and needs to be anchored in hope, humility, and humor.

Be warned: When it comes to life's major stressors, selling your home and moving *even once* lands in the top five stressors along with death, divorce, illness and the loss of a job. The actual process of sorting out your life -- bit by bit, choice by choice -- while pulling your safe and stable "home base" out from under your feet (and out from under your beloved and equally stressed out family and pets) is bound to be frightening, if not emotionally and physically painful. Like English ivy clinging to brick, your "emotional ivy" – the way you've made your house a home throughout the years – is so pervasive that it affects each aspect of and decision you make about your upcoming move. You'll have to rip that "ivy" out of every nook and cranny and off each surface to which it clings, and that's not easy.

With all of this potential stress and disruption on the line, why do we uproot so often? According to the National Association of REALTORS®(NAR), 4.99 million existing homes were sold as of December 2018. USA Today reports that each year, roughly 40 million Americans, or about 14 percent of the U.S. population, move at least once, according to the U.S. Census Bureau. Americans have always had the can-do, pioneer spirit of moving toward something better while leaving the past in the dust. "Go West, young man" no longer means you get in your wagon and traipse across the country. These days, our lives are more complicated and a move requires a strategic plan before you settle into that new territory.

In our modern society, there are a variety of reasons people decide to close one front door and open another. The U.S. Census Bureau found that the most common reasons for moving include: relocating jobs; wanting to own instead of rent; buying a bigger, better home; needing a more affordable home; and downsizing for those with empty nests. There are also life's "rough spots" including death, divorce, illness and financial upheaval that necessitate the sale of a house, sometimes against our will and always creating even greater emotional duress.

Regardless of the reason, America is a country that is constantly on the move, which means that the sale of a house is something most of us will encounter again and again despite the fact that we vow, "Never again." It's like giving birth. The end justifies the means.

So, maybe you've moved multiple times or this is your first move in a decade or ever. The first step is the decision to uproot and change homes. You'll also need to consider packing the roughly 300,000 items that are located, according to the Los Angeles Times (based on statistics cited by professional organizer Regina Lark, Ph.D), in most American homes. Whatever your reason – space, location, budget, life change – it has been decided. Buckle up! This momentous decision is a life changer, and it will place you on a roller coaster from the day you sign a listing agreement with a real estate agent, to the moment you put your feet up at the new house and enjoy that first cup of coffee. Prepare to be pushed beyond your normal limits of endurance emotionally, financially, and physically.

What do I mean by this?

Emotionally: Just say the word "moving" and almost immediately, you're on emotional overload, perhaps without even knowing it. At first, leaving your "old life" sounds exciting thanks to the lure of new beginnings, but then the sentiment rushes in. You're remembering the happy times that transpired within those walls or rewinding to your not-so-thrilling past that took place under that roof. Your emotions are swirling in every direction because that home sheltered you throughout the good times and the bad. It's your home base and safety zone. Questions run through your head: How can a human being divorce itself from bricks and mortar? What happens to that emotional ivy we have grown and now covers the inside and outside of our home? Is this the right move? Does this make good, solid financial sense? Will life be better...over there? Fear of the unknown begins to creep in. Our attachment to the place we call home is rooted as deeply as that prized maple tree in the front yard. You know, the one you planted as a sapling and soon won't be yours anymore.

The journey to your next home involves maximum emotional exposure and an uncomfortable, mind-boggling loss of control. Invaders are everywhere, turning keys and walking around like they own the place (and maybe they soon will). That nice real estate agent is suddenly insisting that no one buys brown exteriors, so please paint it white. (It has always been brown; Your Dad painted it!) The home stager wants you to pack up all your personal photos and mementos – the things that helped make your house a home. Those first few buyers and *lookie-loo* neighbors, who aren't your biggest fans anyway, are suddenly opening your drawers and invading your personal space – and this just feels wrong. It will noticeably sting when that supposedly nice couple traipses through your living room and she whispers, "Those rugs are hideous and who picked those curtains? We'll have to rip everything out!" *Ouch!* Welcome to the home transition emotional roller coaster! Your ride is just beginning and will continue with scary loops, twists, and dizzying falls until it's all over and you are in your new home.

Financially: Let's face it, you have no idea how much this is all going to cost. Changing homes in expensive. Perhaps you have a real estate agent who does a quick walk-through and hands you a laundry list of costly but "required" home improvements. You wake up in the middle of the night in a full sweat, heart beating rapidly. *Seriously?* It will cost $7,000 to paint the entire house and another $4,000 for new flooring and carpeting? And yes, that bathroom leak that you "just sort of live with" will need to be repaired, which includes destroying the wall, replacing the old pipe, and adding a new tile floor.

All of a sudden, you wonder: Is all this really necessary to sell my house? Do I have the money to make these changes now in the *hope* that this investment will bear fruit later in the ultimate sales price? What did the real estate agent say about pulling up all the tired-looking grass and planting fresh sod? *Really?* The roof has how many leaks? And (gulp) how much will it cost to repair? And you haven't even *thought* about the cost of the physical move itself. Is it possible to just close your eyes, hide your credit cards, and wake up when it's all over… and you're in your new home? (Answer: No, but you can wish).

Physically: Right about now, you'll wish you had kept up your gym membership because the act of moving your life from Point A to Point B is a physical one. Even if you don't plan on "doing the heavy lifting," you'll inevitably find yourself bending, stretching, and carrying boxes because moving is a marathon of human endurance, agility, and strength, not limited to moving day. Packing and moving is and has always been a bone-aching, muscle-screaming, physically exhausting production that goes on …and on…and on… for weeks. Yes, you can hire people to help, but like it or not, you will find yourself lugging donation boxes out to the garage, digging through your old closets, and crouching down trying to make some sense out of the lower kitchen cabinets. It didn't feel like much at the time, but you'll feel it later when your back and knees are throbbing in pain.

At this point, you might think, "Okay, it's all a pain, but I know how to move my things from Point A to Point B" and you probably do. But the truth is, you don't know what you don't know, which is one of the reasons I wrote this book. **Based on my 14 years of experience, the key to successfully transitioning homes is to break away from the old ways of thinking. Consider the sale of the home and the move as one continuous process rather than two, separate, unrelated events.** By understanding this approach, and by following the steps detailed in this book, you will understand the inevitable challenges and meet them head on. You'll need real facts, proven solutions, and a plan that doesn't drain your wallet. You also need someone who understands exactly what to do and how to visually and physically package (and pack) your home to sell.

Enter your personal home transition expert.

Me.

I promise to be with you every step of the way offering you my best advice, tips, and proven expertise and information when it comes to this long, arduous process. I want to guide you, the seller, through this journey with the truthful information needed to make educated decisions that lead to meaningful actions. I want to remove the mystery and uncertainty from this process, and replace it with accurate information and actionable steps that will prepare you to transition with confidence and allow you to make the best decisions for you and your family. I will highlight the steps and the process, which are common across all price points. I will guide you through the entire process to strategically master your time and recommend exactly where to invest your money to create a profitable sale and smooth transition to your next home.

I'm Caroline Carter, founder and CEO of the Washington, D.C. Metro area-based business, Done In a Day, Inc. I have over 14 years of hands-on experience in one of the most expensive and competitive housing markets in the country. While serving thousands of clients over many years, I have designed and perfected the Total Home Transition^{SM} (THT) process to address what you, the seller, will face when transitioning your home and your life. My job as a home transition expert is to partner with agents and to guide sellers to make key decisions on what needs to be done in order to sell a house for top dollar. During the process, I work with sellers as they decide what to keep, sell, donate or dump when it comes to those 300,000 personal belongings and which updates are critical to improve the visual value of their home. I acknowledge sellers' fears and feelings of dread at the prospect of what lies ahead and will provide practical advice and clear direction to avoid the common pitfalls while offering the best hacks in the staging and moving industry.

This book was written for you, the sellers and your real estate agents, so you can collaborate on the process of selling your house in a more positive, financially equitable, and mutually beneficial way. This book provides real world answers for an industry that is in flux, with the introduction of companies such as Open Door, iBuyers, Redfin and Houwzer challenging the "old" ways and providing you with new options that may be more financially beneficial to you.

Regardless of which option you choose to sell your house, no one person or agent can currently answer the most critical question for you with pinpoint accuracy: What is the probability (1-100 percent) that you will sell my house in X period (days, weeks, months) of time for X dollars (min, mid or max price)? Since they cannot answer this question, ever, it's up to you, the seller, to take greater responsibility for and control of the process that affects your bottom line the most when it comes to the sale of your asset.

It's key to recognize each person's unique role and responsibility during this transition.

A quick rundown: Real estate agents are expected to sell. Sellers are expected to bear the entire preparation of the house and take all of the financial risks while the agent gets paid a commission regardless of ultimate sales price. Sellers are the ones who are truly knee-deep in this major life transition. And, there really is no one to partner with you throughout the entire transition process which is one of the reasons I started my company. But the truth is, even if you have a great agent, they typically don't get involved in the nitty gritty details of getting the house ready to sell, and they don't help with your move out or your move in. I do.

Let's get back to you. You decide to sell your house and move, and for better or worse, you feel in control and motivated to go through the process...at least for a few days. Then the anxiety and confusion sets in. You begin to doubt your ability to make good quality decisions, and will typically reach out to a real estate agent for help to begin the process. Every successful agent will want to help you understand the sales process, but will also have questions of their own: How soon can you get the house ready to list? Are you willing and able to move out and pay to stage the house? Panic sets in. You begin to realize that your agent, who is supposed to serve you (the seller) first, seems to focus solely on the house sale rather than considering the entire transition process that you will have to go through over time. You have your own questions: What is the total cost of this entire process, and how do I know I am making the best decisions and not leaving "money on the table"? Few agents are able to answer this question with certainty as your overall transition is not their focus. Their focus is the successful marketing and sale of your home. Agents will also benefit by learning the process I will detail in this book to help educate their sellers while ensuring their own successes. A true partnership. You have a different relationship with your home transition expert.

Our partnership begins the moment you decide to sell your home and continues through the move and the unpacking of your new home. I've worked with sellers and their agents in every economic bracket. I've helped move people whose former residences range from 1,500 square foot condos to $15 million mansions. What these sellers have in common is the recognition that they need dedicated emotional and physical support to navigate the complex process of home transition. They also need comparative financial data to weigh the options for choices they will make that affect their bottom line. They've got it. I'm by their side to help them sort and pack their household goods, stage their current house, supervise the move and movers, and strategically unpack them as they begin a new chapter of their lives under a new roof.

I've been there – surrounded by boxes, hopes and fears. I've made many life-changing decisions that involved renting, selling, and yes, moving. I started out as a young woman filling black Hefty trash bags and laundry baskets when I high-tailed it from New Jersey to Massachusetts, finally settling in Washington, D.C. by way of North Carolina, Illinois (twice) and Connecticut. My moves were made both as a single professional and as a married mother of three young children who filled a 53-foot truck as we relocated to the Nation's Capital. There was another move from our family home to a rental for two years after I was divorced. Finally, I moved with my kids to our forever home of the last eleven years.

As I write this book, I'm thinking about 3M ScotchBlue painter's tape and black Sharpies again. Yes, I'm getting ready to begin the transition process soon as my kids are now 18, 20 and 22. It's time to downsize.

So, you could say that I'm right there with you.

The Purpose of This Book

This book is about successful strategy. It will provide the bridge you will need to cross to get from here to there. **SMART MOVES** will help you understand and address the common questions and issues you will face on the road to your new address including: How do I pack up a lifetime? Where do I start? Who do I call? What do I do first? This book will serve as a how-to guide when it comes to your own home sale and move. I will be your personal home transition partner on this emotional, financial and physical journey.

This book will unbundle the TRUE COST of transition when changing homes while providing a unique perspective that combines the preparation to sell and the move in one fluid process.

I am your emotional partner and financial advocate to ensure that you avoid the common pitfalls and mistakes throughout this process. So, whether this is your only home and largest asset or one of several you may own, let's proceed with conviction and determination to make this life change as transparent and painless as possible. Together, we are unbeatable.

This book is organized from soup to nuts, beginning as I do on each project with the initial assessment through unpacking the last box in your new home. Along the way, we'll address the truth about perfection in presentation, evaluating and dealing with moving companies, critical home repairs and touching and evaluating each of your personal "artifacts" gathered over your lifetime. I'll also offer you my **SMART MOVE** tips – actionable suggestions designed to create the visual buyers expect, while saving you time and money to reduce your stress level.

Congratulations! You are on your way to a new life. You have just made your first **SMART MOVE**: You purchased this book for a fraction of the cost of an in-person consultation.

Don't feel discouraged that you need or want help. It's common not to know much about the real estate or moving industries. You are not alone in your fear and anxiety about the sale of your existing home and move into a new abode. On the pages of this book, I'll explain what you need to know to navigate these industries as you deal with the emotional, financial, and physical aspects of this transition.

No one escapes the moving process as its universal no matter where you live, what you're packing or where you're going. There is no way around the process of moving . . . *only through it.*

Are you ready to get moving? Trust the expert? Let the transition begin.

Chapter One

My Smart Moves

My original home base was in Tinton Falls, New Jersey, a borough of Monmouth County known for wildlife trails, horse farms, beautiful parks and decent public schools. I'll always remember my father waking up at sunrise every day to catch the train from Red Bank into New York City. He made that commute for 35 years. Now, many families would just move closer, but those were different times and my parents, who are New York City natives, wanted their four children to grow up in what they called the "country." We were happy there. I was the third child of four with a father who worked in finance and a mother who was an artist, opera singer and exquisite gardener.

We had a lot of property surrounding our house and thinking back I am still struck by our "curb appeal." My mother had created extensive gardens with something blooming year-round, which made it lush and beautiful no matter the season. I was keenly observant of my surroundings. As a child, I was naturally organized, detail-oriented, responsible, kind and thoughtful. A perfectionist from an early age, I focused on cleaning, organizing and beautifying my personal space. I guess Mom's artistic genes rubbed off on me. I was also a hard worker who started babysitting as a "mother's helper" for 50 cents an hour when I was eight years old. By age 12, I was making 75 cents an hour and had $400 in the bank.

While I was studying at Rutgers College in New Brunswick, N.J., I spent a year in Paris at the Sorbonne where I lived with a land-rich, cash-poor Count, Countess and their three teenage kids. Luckily, my years of high school French were passable, which allowed me to speak like a three-year-old child in a foreign language. Quickly, I became fluent enough to avoid the constant teasing, huge bouts of laughter and replies in English that ensued each time I opened my mouth. I was fortunate because both my parents believed that a European year abroad was both an education and an opportunity. Throughout my childhood, there were wonderful trips during which our entire family explored Europe and was exposed to stunning music, art, architecture and culture in Rome, Paris and London.

My First Transition

After graduating college with a Bachelor of Science in Psychology and a minor in French, I had no definitive direction in my life except to get it started, so I headed to Wall Street to join my brothers, Buddy and Philip. Why not? It was the mid-1980s and working in finance was a total blast, or so I understood. I lived in Hoboken, N.J. for two years and dated a young man from a family that ours had known for several generations. Life was good. I had a great job, full social life and the perfect boyfriend, yet I was not truly satisfied or settled. I was feeling a bit restless and unsure about what to do about this when my oldest brother Buddy suggested that we meet for a drink after work.

"I'm really envious of all of you," I told him, concerning my siblings. "All of you went away to college and I stayed in New Jersey."

He said the magic words.

"Why don't you move somewhere?"

Just like so many of my future clients, I did the old "should I, could I" dance. It's always easier to just stay put if given the choice, but wanderlust was nagging at me. "I can't move!" I told him. "Where would I go?"

"Where do you want to go?" he asked.

"I want to go to Boston," I blurted out, never having spent time there.

"So, what's stopping you?" he said

"I don't have the money," I said and immediately felt relief as this was a great excuse not to turn my life upside down.

"OK, consider yourself having six months' rent in the bank," he said. True to his word, as always, he put cash in my account and now I had the ability to change my life. And I did.

I made the decision to move and began the first of many home transitions I would make during my life.

With six months of rent tucked securely in the bank and no job on the immediate horizon, I packed my belongings into black Hefty trash bags and laundry baskets and drove to Bean Town where I lived with my brother's college roommate Scottie and his girlfriend, Lynn, while working in a deli for the summer. I also joined Scottie and his crew and painted houses. By autumn, I took a job as a recruiter for a temp services agency until I went to work for Berlitz, training executives who needed to pick up a foreign language. Shortly after taking the job, I was relocated to Raleigh, North Carolina. After two years, I was asked to move again and spent three years in the Windy City where I was promoted and happily worked (and worked and worked). I finally requested a transfer to the D.C. office to be closer to family.

After several months in D.C., I was sent on a short-term assignment to Stamford, Connecticut where I met my husband on a blind date. He took a job in Chicago, so it was back to Illinois for five and a half years. Each move became more complex with a sea of boxes and furniture as far as the eye could see. When did I go from filling the back of my car when I moved in those carefree younger days to barely squeezing everything into a 53-foot moving truck with 450 boxes?

Three beautiful kids later and we moved to Washington D.C. to be closer to our families. Again.

Our young family and gorgeous home was about to go through major emotional, financial, and physical change. After a few short years in D.C., we divorced, and I knew that I needed to return to work to allow the kids and me to stay in this desirable, but expensive area. I had to ask myself: *What are my strengths?* I started Caroline's Designs, hiring myself out for $50 an hour to do anything organizational or home-related. It was a tough transition in many ways. Start with the fact that I hadn't worked outside the home in 12 years and was a mother of three little kids, ages four, six and eight.

One day, my phone rang, and a unique opportunity was presented to me. Could I help my sister Christina's college roommate transition homes? She had just unexpectedly lost her husband and was raising two small children, ages seven and four. "I can't live in our San Francisco house. There are too many memories," she told me. She needed help to start a new life in a house in Washington D.C. that she had just purchased, sight unseen.

"No problem," I said. "Just send the truck."

Gulp.

In D.C., I quickly sourced the experts needed to help update the new house including replacing carpeting, painting the walls and installing new lighting fixtures for this family with broken hearts. I knew that this had to be special. This poor little boy, who just lost his father, needed joy in his life. I worked with a contractor to build a reading nook in a loft space in his new bedroom as a surprise.

Eventually, their 53-foot moving truck arrived, and I was full steam ahead. I hired a few people to help to unpack and organize the entire house, garage, and storage area. By the time the family arrived in D.C. several days later, their new home was ready and waiting for them along with a huge smile, fresh flowers and hot tea.

The family was thrilled and so was I.

I had rediscovered my natural strengths and abilities while finding my new direction, which was helping others transition one of the most important aspects of their lives: Home base. At the end of that project, my first client said, "Caroline, you should be a home stager. You would be so successful." Then she added, "I would be happy to introduce you to the number two stager in San Francisco who just staged our house for sale."

I had never heard the term *home staging*, but excitedly took his phone number. After a 45-minute phone call, my focus was clear. I would stage homes to sell. This first project led to calls from neighbors and friends who wanted me to stop by their homes and "diagnose" what needed to be done to sell and then help them move into their new homes. There were even people who were staying in their current homes who called and asked me to come over.

"I just hate the way my family room looks," I heard.

"The problem is your sofa is in the wrong place," I'd reply.

"How did I not know this?" the homeowner would marvel.

"I grew up with a creative mother who would change the house to fit the seasons," I replied, explaining how I got my "eye." "Spring meant filmy drapes and winter was taking the slip covers off the furniture." (My mother once asked our pediatrician: "How do I teach my children beauty?" He replied, "You don't. You surround them with it.")

With that natural "good eye," I innately understood color, furniture positioning, decluttering, and the difference between quality and a cheap knockoff at an early age, and believe me, I'm not knocking the knock-off.

I learned from my mother how to strategically create order out of chaos and how to achieve a high-end look for less. These were all very important qualities for success in a developing industry that was about to re-define the process of visually packaging our homes to sell.

After doing extensive research online and locally, I took a course on home staging and put out my shingle for Done In a Day in March of 2005. Home staging was not a widely known term or a commonly used service offered by agents to their sellers at that time in the area, even though it was widely used in California, Canada, and various other parts of the country.

The first three years were spent speaking with the D.C. Metro area's real estate offices and educating agents on exactly what the process entailed and the benefits to them and their clients. As "gatekeepers" for their sellers, they needed to be able to discuss the costs and benefits of the services to explain the process of staging the home to sell at top dollar and to reduce the number of days on the market.

Sellers gravitated toward Done In a Day as a way to make sense of the entire sales cycle and have support during what some knew to be a mind-boggling process. Word spread to their friends as clients recommended me – the truth teller with a concrete plan. My business grew quickly by word-of-mouth referrals and repeat requests for staging from the area's top producing agents and savvy sellers.

It soon became clear to me that most agents have a lot on their plates and getting involved in home staging wasn't something they had the time, expertise, or inclination to do. Why bother? Houses always sell eventually and this was not a widely recognized or utilized sales tool in the D.C. Metro area yet. I explained that designing to sell is actually an art, and it required a more intensive period of time with the client. It was also about saving that seller as much time and money as possible. I've always believed in Home Depot as the top resource to revamp that tired upstairs hallway bathroom for a few thousand dollars versus $10,000 at a specialty kitchen and bath store.

It wasn't long before I got the reputation of being able to do things very quickly, easily, and with fiscal responsibility. Slowly, I built up my crew, hiring the most qualified design assistants, contractors, landscapers, plumbers, painters and other home experts that I could find. They were expected to do a perfect job every single time, and they have. All these years later, we shake our heads that this core team has been together since 2005.

In the beginning, I focused on staging high-end, vacant homes and rented a 6,000 square foot warehouse to store the furniture and accessories I personally curated and used daily. During the financial housing crisis of 2008, when homes weren't selling as rapidly or at all, I did have to reassess my five-year plan, only to realize that with three kids, I needed a more reliable income source. Against my better instincts, but at the repeated suggestion of others who knew me, I got my real estate license in D.C. /Maryland/Virginia and went to work at a small firm but wasn't happy. Unlike with staging, the results were not immediate. Four months later, the managing broker sat me down and said, "We know you're not enjoying this job." Shortly after, during our "spring break vacation " in June because travel was cheaper in summer months, my kids came to me and said, "Mom, we think you should go back to Done In a Day. You were so much happier."

I went back to doing what I love and was good at ... but with a twist. I focused more on the total home transition, not just the preparation and staging of the house. Now, I included the move portion of the process. This was a natural progression with clients who had placed their trust in me from the beginning and it worked beautifully. Clients were willing to pay for this service because it made their lives so much easier emotionally, financially and even physically. They appreciated that I am, above all, a truth teller. I don't waste people's time. I'm kind but firm and, I told them exactly what needed to be done during each phase of the transition and ensured that it was done.

I've built this business over the years for my families -- my own little family with three kids, and the expanded family we have created with the many design assistants, project managers and vendors that serve the needs of our clients. In the early years while I focused on growing this referral-based business, the crews picked up the slack when I couldn't be there by mothering my emotionally fragile kids, cooking, cleaning, and taking care of the house while I focused on finding work to support us all. After two years in a rental home post-divorce, I found a beautiful older home in Bethesda, Maryland.

The house was a fixer-upper built in 1959, which meant we had to get to work. The team used to revamp the house included my contractors and workers, plus the kids and me. Together, we filled eight, 30-yard dumpsters and created a newly renovated space in eight short weeks. We gutted the kitchen and bathrooms and installed new hardwood floors. I was hit with $30,000 for new electrical updates, but as much as it hurt financially, I created what we referred to as our forever home. Once the house was finished, my whole Done In a Day family helped us pack up, move, and place that last glass in the perfect spot in the kitchen cabinets. It has been a house filled with love, warmth and safety and continues to be for myself, and my children who are now 22, 20 and 18.

Was moving on painful for me?

Not really.

I used the same Total Home Transition℠ process I'll describe on the following pages.

Chapter Two

It's Not About You

It starts with a phone call to my office. A REALTOR® (capitalized because they are members of and accountable to the National Association of REALTORS®) is on the other end of the line and will say, "Caroline, I have a seller who really needs your help. We need to schedule a consultation." Does that mean that the home that's about to go on the market is a disaster? No. Almost everyone who goes through the home sale process needs help in at least one of the areas that will be discussed in future chapters. Agents do understand this and many offer to cover the cost of the consultation to provide guidance and clear direction to prepare the house to list on the MLS (Multiple Listing Service) as it is known around the country. The MLS is the service used for real estate brokers to share information about properties listed for sale.

Word-of-mouth from past successes also brings sellers directly to me. I frequently hear, "My home has been on the market for two months and we've had some traffic, but no offers. I'm freaking out. I close on my new home in a month." Or maybe it's a case of an overwhelmed individual who is hyperventilating *just thinking about selling.* "I'm paralyzed and can't even start this process, but the launch date is looming."

Regardless of the situation, I always begin with the consultation. This is the first critical step in the transition process. For under $500, I'll spend as long as it takes, usually an hour or two, to tour a home both inside and out, to discuss how the house aligns with current buyer preferences and to recommend visual and cosmetic updates to close the gap between what the buyer covets and what the seller has to offer.

We discuss the entire journey from Point A to Point B and exactly which steps and critical decisions need to happen along the way. I'll do the same for you, Reader, on the pages of this book starting with the vital fact that selling your house is actually NOT about you, the seller, although it affects you. It's really about the buyer, the person who will be purchasing your house. Or not.

This is crucial: **Your job as the seller is to make sure that your home is delivered in a condition that will allow a qualified buyer up to one year of occupancy without making material changes.** No one wants to move into "an immediate project." Providing this period of 12 months may be the difference between an offer and stagnation on the market thus saving you money, time and emotional stress.

SMART MOVE: Hiring a Realtor instead of a real estate agent is a smart decision. This person will be a member of the National Association of REALTORS® which means they adhere to a strict Code of Ethics that protects clients, the public and other real estate agents.

Let's Begin

The process begins for me when I pull up to your home and immediately rate the visual impact of its current presentation.

As I make my way to the front door, I am mentally taking notes on exactly what issues will need to be addressed should we come to terms and work together. This initial glance at the visual curb appeal may include trimming or even removing that overgrown evergreen that blocks the façade of the house or the maze of small ceramic pots and plants one has to navigate on the front step. I'll mentally jot down that your fence is in good shape, but needs a fresh coat of paint, or a quick power wash.

Wait. I can't see the numbers on the house because they're covered in climbing vines. In a future chapter, I'll explain how to maximize your curb appeal. But for now, it's enough to know that your home will be judged by buyers **the very minute** their feet hit your driveway. I'm just putting myself in their shoes.

Those shoes are on your front porch.

I ring the bell.

The person who answers the door is moving on – happily, unhappily, warily and in most cases, anxiously. Most sellers are overwhelmed with the thought of packing up their belongings even if they're just moving down the street although many are leaving the state or moving far away. They're stressed. Confused. Needing answers to their many questions, but fearful of the bottom line and how much this will cost them.

Recall that we already discussed how your family home is probably your largest financial asset, so it's important to approach this in a logical and business-like way.

I know it's tough. It's about to get tougher.

Before we get into how to stage or maximize the value of the home, I try to understand what's going on inside the minds of the sellers. Every home I enter provides its own unique tale. The decision to sell your home base is not just a financial one, but also a deeply emotional one that sometimes plays out like a mini soap opera.

I'll never forget the 40ish year old Washington woman who sat at that lovely oak kitchen table staring daggers at the husband who was excited to sell their home and move to Florida, while she planned on growing old at their current home. It wasn't so much a case of: Can this real estate transaction be saved? It was more: Can this marriage be saved? (I didn't realize that I was doing marriage counseling, but sometimes it comes with the territory).

"I don't really want to sell the house where I raised the children," she insisted.

"But it's crazy to stay in this big house with the high taxes. And, did you see last month's electric bill?" he retorted.

And on it went for our entire meeting. Both of them just stared at me when I began to make suggestions. The Realtor told me that they weren't exactly "open" to change, so I was aware of this before the meeting. "How can you possibly ask me to remove the yellow paint that I love in my kitchen? My daughter picked out that color," the woman asked me when I suggested a neutral beige tone.

"I will not take family photos off the walls," she scoffed. "Buyers will have to look past our things, which are staying up until the day I leave this house. I can't go a day without looking at our photos."

This is where the powerful emotional attachment to our homes becomes an issue. It wouldn't be *her* kitchen for long although the acceptance of that fact hadn't sunk in yet. And no, buyers wouldn't look past the 100 or more photos in old mismatched frames that made the hallways look cluttered and claustrophobic. They would need to be removed to showcase hallways that were actually narrow in the first place. And the truth is she *could* survive a month or two without reliving that trip to Greece in 1982.

I have to remind sellers of a simple, but true real estate fact: **It's not about YOU. It's about BUYERS,** and they are in the driver's seat. In fact, today's buyers have a preference for visual and physical perfection and style whether it's traditional, modern or transitional. We live in a visually overstimulated world where the standards of judgement are often high and unrealistic. **That said, your next job as the seller is to present a house as visually close to what current buyers expect and are determined to find. This dictates that changes within your home will almost certainly need to be made to create a modern, up-to-date listing that appeals to a wide cross section of potential buyers.**

One of the first action items to achieve that listing and successful sale is that you (the seller) must strip the emotion out of the process. Rather than approaching the sale of your home with fear, nostalgia or even anger, step out of the emotional quicksand. Again, this is not about you and your memories. This is about money and where you will need to spend it to sell for top dollar.

Once you remove the emotion and view the house as an asset, it becomes easier to get the ball rolling and logically prepare your home for sale in a way that will generate immediate interest. No, that doesn't always mean ripping out all the floors downstairs or spending $10,000 or more on new windows. On the following pages, I have more cost-effective fixes and ways to work around pressing visual "issues."

I'll never forget the seller who laughed when I purchased fairly inexpensive black vinyl shutters from Home Depot and had them placed on the front of her two million dollar home. It made the once plain front façade pop and the offers rolled in. Originally, this lovely lady balked and told me, "But it doesn't look like my house with those shutters. I don't like it. I'm the one who took off the shutters years ago when I moved in!"

Vinyl shutters up! *Finito!*

Here's the point: The colonial style house needed additional visual definition and those shutters were the appropriate, affordable solution. All the houses on the block had them and this particular house looked odd and out of place without them. And, deep breath, she didn't have to like it because she wasn't going to live there. This wasn't about personal taste, it was a **SMART MOVE** to sell the home. Take the emotion out of this process -- easy to say and hard to do. Get on board at the start to understand the importance and impact of visually packaging your home to sell in order to save time and money.

Back to the home assessment, which is why I'm here. I observe sellers' defensive body language and note the expression of fear on their faces as they typically greet this invasion of their home. I anticipate this and am prepared for it. It was bad enough when their Realtor quickly walked through the house and mentioned something about painting and maybe replacing some of the floors. No, they don't exactly remember what he said. He didn't write it down. And that's appropriate because a detailed visual and physical home assessment is something that many real estate agents don't have the time or the experience to do in a meaningful or deep way. Yes, your agent might give you a few broad strokes such as you'll need to slap a new coat of paint on the inside and invest in a new roof. What they are really saying is how quickly can you have your house ready?

I deal in the details and provide affordable solutions.

My staging recommendations are factual, based on years of experience working with over 2,000 sellers, all of whom began the process exactly where you are now. Buyer preferences have changed over time, but the process of designing to sell has not. I understand what current buyers expect and you should, too. For example, they don't want lilac walls, but do appreciate the wider crown molding. Those hardwood floors can stay with a buffing, but that oversized hot tub or mold factory outdoors needs to be hauled away.

From this day forward, think of your house like a product. A product that you and your agent are selling, together. You will design that product so that it stands out from its competition and "speaks" to buyers in a meaningful way. The visual value we will create will increase the probability of selling your house faster and for top dollar so that you can move on with the next phase of your life.

Salesperson. Product. Sell.

You have a job to do.

The Good, the Bad and the Not-So-Ugly

It's actually quite simple. You need to ensure that when a highly qualified buyer views your well-maintained and presented home and property that they can imagine themselves living there. This is why it's critical to do a realistic visual assessment of your home and the property surrounding it. **Your buyer wants and needs a year of living** comfortably, neutrally, and in 100 percent stain-free, odor-free space with all appliances in good, working order. This is my Gold Standard.

Here are a few examples:

House Number 1: Purple, yellow and green paint on the walls.

Can they live with it for a year? The answer is most people would lose their minds.

House Number 2: Neutral beige walls with classic white trim.

Can they live with it for a year? Absolutely. It may not be their personal preference, but it's fine for now and will show well to friends and family who can't wait to see the new house.

House Number 3: Old carpeting throughout the house that has tell-tale pet stains and dirty spots although it was professionally cleaned.

Can they live with it for a year? No. Who wants to buy someone else's smells and dirt?

House Number 4: New, neutral gray carpeting and engineered wood floors throughout the house.

Can they live with it for a year? Yes. Again, it is not their taste. They want real hardwood floors, but that can wait a year.

House Number 5: Kitchen has old countertops with small white tiles and mostly clean grouting.

Can they live with it for a year? Not really. The counter is chipped and makes the kitchen look like the '90s are back again.

House Number 6: Appliances aren't top of the line in the kitchen, but they are clean and operational. New granite countertops.

Can they live with it for a year? Yes, that kitchen remodel will happen someday, but for now, it is perfectly functional.

My all-important "live with it for a year" standard is what will

get you that fast sale at top dollar because few buyers are looking for a major home renovation project. Yet, I sit with sellers who try to rationalize, "But the buyer will change it anyway. Why do I have to put new carpeting in?" The truth is that they will eventually change it out, but for now and those 12 months following the move, they just want to live without Fifi's former litter box accidents. Wouldn't you?

Meet the Gold Standard of those 12 months and your home will rise to the top of most "must-see" lists. Sure, eventually the buyer will renovate the galley kitchen and install the chef's kitchen of their dreams, but they don't have to do it before they move in. What exactly constitutes those 12 months? Working appliances, neutral paint, new carpeting, updated or refinished floors, light fixtures and doors and windows that work without needing special instructions. Those are just a few items on my list that we will delve into in the next chapters.

Just the other day, I was with sellers whose house was going to list at $1.2 million. "There are a few little things that are a bit out of sorts," the top business executive told me. "The back-patio sliding door is made of wood – which is now warped – but the new people can deal with it. You can't really open it now, but I'm not spending the $4,000 to have a new custom door made." Yes, he will have to replace it, but possibly not for that much cash. I've got a "guy."

Same buyer and I wandered down into their basement to the "laundry room." It was not a separate room, but a dark corner of the partially finished basement. It was like walking into a horror show of furniture sent to die and where their pets went to the bathroom regularly. Again, these issues don't provide the year your buyers want and need. **No one will want to pay for your issues, unless they chip away at the list price until they can justify the cost and the work it will take to make it "livable".**

By the way, it's not enough to have a killer first floor with a mess upstairs and downstairs. Today, basements or lower level family rooms need to be multi-functional and provide clean and clear storage, perhaps even a lower level pantry and a gift-wrapping station. So much for shag carpeting, fake paneling and lava lamps!

To Spend or Not to Spend

My job is to be the truth teller; and I like to tell the truth early and often. I am the real estate agent's secret weapon. I tackle the sensitive issues about the house that the agent would prefer not to discuss so that they can remain positive and focused on locating a buyer. Often, the sellers have a financial budget in mind to sell their home based on a figure that they can "afford", and feel is "fair." I've learned to expect this because no one wants to spend money on a home they're leaving, but this budget is rarely based on the actual work that needs to be done to sell the house.

Knee-jerk negativity to my recommendations typically relates more to an arbitrary or uninformed budget rather than the actual recommendations themselves. I address it immediately. These recommended areas of improvement are physical issues that will not pass the required home inspection, nor will they pass a buyer's visual inspection. These problems are often referred to as "delayed maintenance." They are certain to register negatively with a potential buyer who will express their lack of serious interest by quickly moving on to view the next listing.

My job is to know what creates value in the mind of today's buyer and educate you on which areas of the home to highlight and which may be considered a liability in its current visual or physical state. The recommendation list I create during my tour with you is based on a visual "scorecard" of the home from its front door curb appeal, moving back inside the home and then into the yard. This list will help you determine where your hard-earned dollars are best spent. You will learn how to evaluate your own list to fit your budget by following the tools I'll give you in the upcoming chapters.

In a seller's mind, his or her objective is simple: I want to sell my house as quickly as possible for the highest possible price, spend the least amount of money and do the least amount of work. The buyer's objective is *also* simple: I want to buy the best possible house as quickly as possible, for the best possible price, do the least amount of work and spend the least amount of money.

Do you see the problem?

You're at opposite ends of a complex spectrum. What my Total Home Transition^{SM} process does is to bring seller and buyer closer together in terms of current wants and needs. I'll do whatever I have to do to highlight the assets of a room from ripping up old carpeting to reveal the hardwood floor underneath to playing up those gorgeous high ceilings by painting them white. At the same time, I'll work hard to deflect the eye from any visual or physical liabilities as we shine a light on what's unique about the property without making cost-prohibitive changes.

The number one question on most sellers' minds when it comes to staging: Does it have to be expensive?

Answer: Absolutely not.

The other day I walked into a house that had an odd-shaped foyer. On the East Coast, buyers love to wander into a spacious foyer that sets the tone for a luxury home. This one didn't need new expensive flooring as was suggested by their Realtor. The problem was that the sellers had a gorgeous maple chest and mirror, but the pair was placed on the wrong wall, a wall that needed a fresh coat of paint. All we had to do is move the furniture and repaint the walls, and suddenly the space looked entirely different and showed beautifully.

In another center hall colonial, the seller was nervously waiting to hear from me if she needed pricey new window treatments in the living room. Yes, the floral ones she had for years were old, sun-damaged, dusty and made the room look smaller. However, we did not need to purchase anything new to update the style and showcase the windows and filtered light. In the end, we took the floral window treatments down and left the neutral colored sheers in place that were hung underneath the drapes. It was a low-cost solution that made the room look twice as large and beautifully complimented a fresh and inexpensive coat of neutral paint.

Basta!

SMART MOVE: Focus on your own unique house. It's your ASSET and worth the most money to you. It is ultimately up to you to decide the list price. Let your real estate expert provide the available data, guidance and feedback to help price your house, but keep an open mind. You need to work together, non-emotionally, to arrive at a price point that reflects the value of the bricks and mortar that you are selling.

A Quick Story: Christmas In May

I did a consultation last year with a woman who had three kids, a big dog and a bigger house. She was a life coach…who needed a life coach. It looked like a bomb had gone off *inside the house*. Her regular world was so busy and out of control and her house *looked* like her daily schedule was packed! Not to rat her out, but this woman's Christmas tree was in the corner of the living room. *And it was May!* She was quick to mention that it was a family joke. I wondered.

"We're thinking of moving, but we have to sell this house first," she told me. "In fact, we want to get it on the market by Friday." (That was three days away). After completing a two-hour interior and exterior consultation, she ended up entering what I call "the manic phase." She couldn't believe that there were a few weeks of real work to prepare the house to list and her family to move. I strongly suggested she address the "fixes" we had identified before listing…and that this didn't need to be costly, but it should be done to get as much money out of her home as possible. She told me that she needed every dollar for her new house. Again. Meanwhile, her agent had paid my consultation fee because he knew that she needed my help, and he wanted to the house to sell quickly for top dollar. A few days went by after our consultation, and I called the agent to see if the woman had any questions. Her feedback was simple: "No, I don't have questions. I'll do everything myself."

She decided that she didn't need my help, but at least she had my recommended updates list. There are consultations that end that way and I don't end up working with the client. I forgot all about this woman until a month later when I looked at the listing on the MLS. Her house had been listed for weeks and there was only one picture there, which was the exterior photo of her house. (Always a red flag to buyers! You might have just written: Beware!) It was still showing "active."

Hmmm. No surprise there.

In the end, the house sat on the market for three months until it finally sold for tens of thousands of dollars less than her asking price.

Back to the Beginning: It's About the Buyer

Here is a simple key to buyers: They will walk through your house and give themselves less than ten minutes to decide if this could be "it". Many will only devote four or five minutes and make a snap decision -- yes or no. This means that they will fly through your rooms in less than a minute or two and if they are distracted and a few things seem odd or cause them to pause and question, you've lost their attention. They're on their phones urging their Realtor to find more listings.

Ask yourself (and be honest): What will buyers see and remember in the ten minutes they literally fly through my house deciding if they can imagine themselves living here? Let's find out.

Now, it's time for us to do our initial walk-through in detail.

Chapter Three

Interior Assessment

During the initial interior assessment, we tour each room of the house to look closely at the way the rooms currently present, but from an altitude of 30,000 feet. There is no need to open each drawer and cabinet at this point. We will discuss the importance of overall presentation and identify potential issues that need to be addressed and look for opportunities to make meaningful visual and physical updates throughout the house to create value in the minds of the buyer. We will look at your furniture, carpeting, rugs, lamps, artwork and accessories and discuss ideas of how to use them in new and interesting places.

> **SMART MOVE:** Do a walk-through of your entire house in and out of each room. You need two to two-and-a-half feet to walk comfortably through the rooms without feeling physically or psychology crowded. Clear a natural path to easily navigate without stepping over or side-swiping your things.

It's crucial to understand that most buyers will insist on a home inspection once they have a ratified contract on your house. While a house can't "fail" a home inspection, it can receive a poor "grade" and require the seller to agree to a list of repairs or make financial restitution for these repairs as they scramble to save the sale. If you're concerned about your own house, you might want to schedule a pre-inspection with a certified home inspector now to prepare yourself to address issues that might present a problem later.

SMART MOVE: Review the Sample Pre-Home Inspection Checklist below and determine where you might receive a low grade.

SAMPLE PRE-HOME INSPECTION CHECKLIST:

Grounds:

- ☐ Proper grading away from the house
- ☐ No evidence of standing water
- ☐ No leaks from septic tank or leach field
- ☐ Yard, landscaping, trees and walkways in good condition
- ☐ No branches or bushes touching house or overhanging the roof
- ☐ Exterior structures (fences, sheds, decks, retaining walls, detached garages) in good working condition with no evidence of termite damage or rotted wood
- ☐ Railings on stairs and decks adequate and secure

☐ Driveways, sidewalks, patios, entrance landings in good condition and graded away from structure

☐ Downspout drainage directed away from house

Structure:

☐ Ridge and fascia board lines appear straight and level

☐ Sides of house are straight, not bowed or sagging

☐ Window and door frames are square and not bowed

☐ Visible foundation in good condition with no cracks

Exterior:

☐ Adequate clearing between ground and wood siding materials (6" minimum); no wood-to-earth contact

☐ Wood siding: secure; no cracking, curling, rot or decay

☐ Masonry veneers: no cracks in joints or broken or flaking components

☐ Stucco: no large cracks

☐ Vinyl or aluminum siding: no dents, damage, not bowing or loose siding

☐ No vines on surface of structure

☐ Exterior paint or stain: no flaking or blisters

☐ No stains on exterior

Windows, Doors and Wood Trim:

☐ Wood frames and trim pieces are secure, no cracks, rot or decay

- ☐ Joints around frames are caulked
- ☐ No broken window or storm window panes or damaged screens
- ☐ Windows properly insulated; storm windows or thermal glass in place
- ☐ Muntin and mullion glazing in good condition

Roof:

- ☐ Composition shingles: no curling, cupping, or loss of granulation particulate; no broken, damaged or missing shingles; not more than two layers of roofing
- ☐ Wood shingles or shakes: no mold, rot, decay, cracked/broken/missing shingle or curling
- ☐ Flat roofs: no obvious patches; no cracks, splits or silt deposits; minimal blisters or wrinkles, all flashings sealed with tar
- ☐ Flashing around all roof penetrations
- ☐ No evidence of excess roofing cement/tar/caulk
- ☐ Soffits and fascia: no decay or stains
- ☐ Exterior venting for eave areas: vents clean and not painted over
- ☐ Gutters and downspouts: no decay or rust; joints sealed; securely attached to house; no missing sections; clean, no mud deposits
- ☐ Chimneys: straight, properly flashed; no evidence of damaged bricks or cracked joints; mortar/cement cap in good condition

Attic:

- ☐ No stains on underside of roofing
- ☐ No evidence of decay or damage to house
- ☐ Sufficient insulation that's properly installed
- ☐ Adequate ventilation: clear path into attic for air entering through soffit vents, adequately sized gable end louvers, all mechanical ventilation operational
- ☐ No plumbing, exhaust or appliance vents terminating in attic
- ☐ No open electrical splices

Interior Rooms:

- ☐ Floors, walls and ceilings are straight and level
- ☐ No stains on floors, walls, ceilings
- ☐ Flooring materials in good condition
- ☐ No significant cracks in walls or ceilings
- ☐ Windows and exterior doors operate easily and latch properly; have weather stripping; no broken glass, no sashes painted shut, no decay
- ☐ Interior doors operate easily and latch properly; no damage or decay; no broken hardware
- ☐ Paint, wall covering and paneling in good condition
- ☐ Wood trim installed and in good condition
- ☐ Lights and light switches operate properly
- ☐ Adequate number of three-pronged electrical outlets in each room
- ☐ Electrical outlets test properly
- ☐ Heating/cooling source in each room
- ☐ Adequate insulation in walls

☐ Fireplaces: no cracking or damaged masonry, no evidence of smoke staining on fireplace façade, damper operates properly, clean flue

Kitchen:

☐ Working exhaust fan vents to house exterior

☐ Ground Fault Circuit Interrupter (GFCI) protection for electrical outlets within six feet of sink

☐ Dishwasher drains properly, no leaks, door springs operate properly

☐ No leaks in pipes under sink

☐ Cabinet floor under sink is solid, no stains or decay

☐ Water flow in sink adequate

☐ No excessive rust or deterioration on garbage disposal or waste pipes

☐ Built-in appliances operate properly

☐ Cabinets in good condition; doors and drawers operate properly

Bathrooms:

☐ Working exhaust fan that vents to house exterior

☐ Adequate water flow and pressure from all fixtures

☐ Sink, tub and shower drain properly

☐ Plumbing and cabinet floor under sink in good condition

☐ If sink is metal, no sign of rust; overflow drain doesn't leak

☐ Toilet operates properly, no rocking, no stains around base

- ☐ Caulking in good condition inside and outside of tub and shower area
- ☐ Tub or shower tiles secure, wall surface solid
- ☐ No stains or evidence of past leaking around base of bath or shower

Miscellaneous:

- ☐ Smoke and carbon monoxide detectors in good working order
- ☐ Stairway treads and risers solid
- ☐ Stair handrails secure and in good condition
- ☐ Automatic garage door opener operates properly, stops properly for obstacles

Basement:

- ☐ No evidence of moisture
- ☐ Exposed foundation: no stains, no major cracks, no flaking
- ☐ Visible structural wood: no sagging, damage, decay or stains; no damage from insects; secure attachment to foundation with anchor bolts
- ☐ Insulation at rim/band joists

Plumbing:

- ☐ Visible pipes: no damage, evidence of leaks or signs of stains on materials near pipes; drain pipes slope slightly down towards outlet to septic/sewage system

- [ ] Water heater: no rust, vented properly, sized to produce adequate quantity of hot water for the number of bathrooms in the house
- [ ] Water pump does not short cycle.
- [ ] Galvanized pipes do not restrict water flow
- [ ] Well water test is acceptable
- [ ] Hot water temperature is between 118 to 125 degrees Fahrenheit

Electrical:

- [ ] Visible wiring in good condition, no exposed splices, cables secured and protected
- [ ] Service panel: adequate capacity, all cables attached to panel with cable connectors, fuses or breakers are not overheating
- [ ] No aluminum cable for branch circuits

Heating/Cooling System:

- [ ] Appears to operate well throughout with good airflow on forced air systems
- [ ] Flues: no open seams, slopes up to chimney connection
- [ ] No rust around cooling unit
- [ ] No combustion gas odor
- [ ] Air filter(s) clean
- [ ] Ductwork is in good condition
- [ ] No asbestos on heating pipes, water pipes or air ducts
- [ ] Separate flues for gas/oil/propane and wood/coal

INTERIOR OVERVIEW

Your Personal Footprint

What is your personal footprint when it comes to your home? Or perhaps the better question is: What have you done to make that house a home? It could be the gallery of lovely family photos that run the length of the long hallway to the bedrooms or that porcelain figurine collection handed down from generation to generation. Do you have an impressive art collection or blown glass arsenal? People have interesting and personal collections that define their lives, loves and adventures. How you personally design your home to reflect your life is normal and expected...until it comes time to sell your house.

Today's buyers are easily distracted. Instead of focusing on the actual bricks and mortar, they're suddenly intrigued by your personal footprint, asking themselves, "Who lives here? Are they happy? Why are they selling?"

Packing up your personal footprint allows you to offer a clean, de-cluttered, clearly defined blank slate for buyers to clearly see the space they are considering for their own family.

Paint

The overall color scheme in a house makes a huge impact and lasting impression on the buyer. If the rooms are multi-colored and non-neutral, they represent time, money and work that the buyer must undertake and finance before moving into the house. It also becomes a predominant and distracting feature that a buyer will focus on and remember rather than the actual rooms, flow and layout of the house. The paint needs to be neutral with white ceilings and trim. The ideal look is classic, clean and removes seller-specific choices or designer signatures.

⚠️ There should be no water stains, uneven surfaces, settlement cracks, paint bubbles or evidence of prior work when it comes to walls and ceilings. It's equally important to look at the switch plates. Are they mirrored? Painted a funky color? You'll need to paint them in the same neutral wall color so they disappear or replace them with white. A kaleidoscope of wall colors may make your house look dated, although there are always exceptions. In a Georgian colonial, for example, it's not uncommon to see a Chinese red dining room or a hunter green library.

Flooring

Flooring represents another area of critical importance and huge visual and physical impact when selling your house. Sellers need to present floors in almost new condition regardless of type- solid hardwood, engineered hardwood, ceramic and vinyl tile, laminate, linoleum or stone.

⚠️ Wood floors that are excessively scratched, gouged, marred, irrevocably stained or sun damaged. Cracked or missing tile or stone. Peeling linoleum.

Carpeting and Rugs

Carpeting in good condition without obvious wear, stains, fraying or matted edges. Area rugs must be in almost new condition, the right color and style and size proportionate to the room.

⚠ Odor, pet and other non-removable stains. Rugs that overwhelm a room in color and style should be removed to reveal the flooring underneath.

Lighting

Most buyers don't respond well to a dark house; they want a house that's filled with adequate light; natural light, recessed light, lamps (standing and table) and fixtures (chandeliers, wall sconces, and other sources). You must provide enough different light sources for buyers to view your property at any time of the day or night.

⚠ Light-blocking, dated or heavy-looking window treatments. Old, multi-colored metal blinds or blinds that no longer work and block natural light. Uneven distribution of light throughout the rooms due to low wattage or incorrect bulb types. An inadequate number of table or floor lamps.

Artwork and Sculpture

Buyers do appreciate various styles and genres of artwork and sculpture displayed in well-designed homes. This artwork and sculpture are like the "jewelry" used to adorn the room and highlight areas of interest and common placement locations.

⚠ Artwork on every wall throughout the house with little focused thought to placement, proportion, style, color and effect. Oversized or distracting sculptures.

Plant Material

Buyers may or might not admire your green thumb, but they will balk at the idea that you live in a jungle. Live plants and flowers must be in proportion to the area or room in which they are placed and not distracting in number, size or condition.

⚠ A profusion of plants and floral arrangements spread throughout the house that are in varying states of decay - brown leaves or vases with dirty water. Uncontrollable vines and old, dying ficus trees are unacceptable as are plants that take up too much space and light.

Fireplaces

Fireplaces are often *the* focal point of any room. They're a great selling point if in good condition with an updated look.

⚠ Broken or chipped brick or tile, missing mortar, soot-stained, non-working gas components, cracked glass doors, too big or too small mantles or decorative tiles. Burned out black interior, broken damper.

Odor

Buyers want a house that smells fresh, clean and completely non-odorous. If your home has a funky smell from pets, smoke or cooking spices don't ignore it. You are likely immune to the smell of your own home because we all are, so ask others for their honest opinions. Pervasive odor needs to be identified and addressed immediately.

⚠ Common culprits: throw pillows, old rugs, old cutting boards, a funky smelling fridge, moldy closets, old carpeting and pet beds. Smelly bathrooms? It could be a leaky pipe or poor ventilation. Check window frames where condensation builds up and can smell musty.

Foyer/Entrance

Your foyer or entry way is the buyer's first glimpse of the level of design, order and cleanliness you're presenting throughout the house. You will not get a second chance to make a first impression and reset the tone. Buyers should see the width and depth of a well-lit foyer with appropriately sized furniture, mirror and artwork where space permits.

⚠ Oversized or undersized furniture, poor lighting and too much artwork that draws the eye in different directions. Family clutter including mail, keys, shoes, jackets, backpacks, library books and pet leashes.

Living Room

While becoming less important in a transitional-style home, the living room is still a key room in many homes and should feature multiple seating areas if space allows. It should contain a sofa that's proportionate to the size of the room with a rug that's large enough for the main seating area. Furniture should be placed in a visually logical format. Your sofa should be flanked by two side tables with a lamp on each. A proper coffee table, poof or cubes placed in front of your sofa will complete the main seating arrangement.

⚠ Rugs that are too small for the room and an explosion of furniture that's hard to navigate around. Too many accessories on tabletops or an overabundance of artwork, photos and treasures displayed in built-in shelves, cluttering bookcases or on walls.

Dining Room

Buyers will want this room restored to an actual dining room even if you're not using it for that purpose. You will need to show a dining room table, chairs and perhaps a sideboard or china cabinet. If you do not have a sideboard or china cabinet, a sofa table and mirror will illustrate the potential use of extra space. A floral centerpiece on the dining table is a welcome accent.

⚠ Anything that overpowers or distracts the buyer from seeing the square footage of the room, its use and all light sources. Remove or add extra table leaves to highlight room size.

Family/Great Room

This is the relaxation and gathering spot for the family and needs to look like a place where adults and children can watch movies, play games, read or just de-stress.

⚠ Furniture sizes, styles and colors that overwhelm the room, bookshelves that are overly packed with books, personal mementos and clutter.

Kitchen

Buyers expect a kitchen to be clean, serviceable and present an overall design scheme and color that is current. They need neutral walls, functional appliances, under-cabinet lighting and overhead fixtures using the correct type bulbs and wattage. Cabinet doors and drawers must be free of stains and grease or freshly painted with updated knobs and pulls. Flooring must be in good condition and polished or replaced. Countertops should be sealed, stain-free and look serviceable. Window coverings should be minimal and look new or be removed.

⚠ Dark paint on kitchen walls, busy, distracting or cracked backsplash, non-working broken and/or visually mismatched appliances, broken appliance lights and fans, poor lighting, poor ventilation, evidence of cooking grease, odor, dated cabinet color, old drawer pulls and cabinet knobs and misaligned cabinet doors. Cracked, stained or unsealed countertops. Water stains from leaking pipes under the sink.

> **SMART MOVE:** Deep clean and organize your kitchen cabinets and drawers. Take everything out, cabinet by cabinet and drawer by drawer, remove shelf and drawer lining and pack or donate non-necessary items to create space. Gather all warranties and critical house documents the new homeowners will need and place in one drawer.

Master Bedroom

Buyers want a master bedroom that will allow them to de-stress from the world. It should be a calming, spa-like retreat with a warm, neutral wall color. Window treatments should be light filtering and carpeting cleaned or replaced. Ideally, there should be a queen or king-sized bed with two side tables or nightstands with lamps. It's important to see a dresser with a mirror. If there is room for a seating area, there might be a chair or small loveseat with another table and lamp. The closet should be clean, odorless and organized. Built-in bookshelves or cabinets should contain minimal books and decorative accents. A TV is optional.

⚠ Furniture that is not in proportion with the scale of the room. Dark colors, too many patterns and styles in artwork, bedding and furniture. Dirty or tired bedding/pillows. Stained or frayed carpeting. Multiple area rugs over carpeting. Overflowing bookshelves and tables with personal magazines, books and photos.

Bathrooms

Buyers want bathrooms to present like a mini-spa. They must be sparkling clean, fully functional and well lit. In all bathrooms, the sink or vanity, medicine cabinet and lighting should be operative and their hardware should be in a current finish. The showerhead should be rust-free and the bath and the glass shower doors should be crystal clear or removed and replaced with a rod, shower curtain and liner. Old grout and caulk needs to be replaced. Fresh towels should be displayed.

⚠ Chipped, broken, cracked or missing tile and dirty grout and caulking. Cloudy shower doors, old curtains and liners, dated vanity, medicine cabinet, lighting and hardware. Broken or stained toilet seat. Non-working ceiling fan, tub jets or rusted shower head and shower curtains. Shampoo bottles, old razors, bath toys, make-up, stacks of old magazines or books, plus toothbrushes and half-used products on counters or tubs. Litter boxes.

Basement

Buyers are looking for a clean, well-lit and well-defined space. Recently shampooed or new carpeting or flooring. This is typically one of the most re-carpeted rooms in the house when preparing to sell. Bars/kitchens in basements with older appliances and sinks must be clean and functional.

⚠️ Evidence of past water damage, poor overhead lighting, stained carpeting or cracked, broken or missing tile. Cloudy or cracked window panes. Unidentified odor. Unused or half-used building material or the ghosts of projects past.

Laundry Room

Buyers want a washer and dryer in perfect working condition, shelving or cabinets and a clean, functional laundry sink and faucet. Walls painted white, flooring like new, lighting bright and the room completely organized.

⚠️ Non-working appliances, poor ventilation, chipped and stained laundry sink, peeling linoleum or cracked tile floor. Old rags. Lint-covered surfaces. Insufficient lighting and old kitchen cabinets that are in their original color with dated hardware.

Attic/Storage

Buyers need a clean, well-lit space that is available for storage. Buyers should be able to see clearly the width and depth of usable space in one quick glance. Insulation should be tacked securely and neatly into the rafters. No evidence of rodent infestation. Easily accessible windows and HVAC equipment. Working attic fan.

⚠ Unsafe flooring, mouse and rat traps and droppings, evidence or odor of mold and must, falling insulation, poor lighting, leftover building material from completed renovations and gallons of old paint. Anything blocking the windows.

Garage

Lighting adequate to showcase entire usable space. Refrigerators and freezers clean and functional. Shelving can be used for sports equipment, bikes, seasonal storage, landscaping and gardening items, car wash supplies, tools, trash cans and recycling bins. This space can also be used for packed boxes and furniture that is not affected by temperature fluctuations. Consider painting the walls and floor.

⚠ Water-damaged walls, bug or rodent traps, cracked cement walls or floor, poor lighting, broken windows and non-functional garage door.

Don't Jump The Gun

A few years ago, I met with a client who was quite demanding. He was a classic old school, loud, CEO, with a Type A personality who was used to getting what he wanted at work and at home – and fast. He began our consultation by bombarding me with questions (which was fine), but I couldn't help noticing his wife standing meekly behind us with their tiny dog who looked a bit shaken. "Can you please stand in that one spot by the door?" the wife asked me when I entered their house. "The dog is nervous in social situations. We need to allow her to come to you."

Have That "Old House" Smell?

Buyers will quickly run away from a house that has an "old house" smell. This isn't created by older people living in the home, but is the result of little ventilation, high humidity in many cases, and darkness. Scientifically speaking, you're smelling MVOC: Mold Volatile Organic Compounds or chemicals in the mold life cycle that evaporate and cause an odor (which isn't the same as health-threatening mold). You can get rid of the smell by opening windows to air out the house and then running the air conditioning colder than room temperature to get rid of humidity in the air. Professionally clean upholstered furniture, which traps this smell, and doing the same with carpets can also rid the house of that funky smell. In addition, cleaning your air ducts can also do the trick.

It wasn't just the dog. Everyone in the house seemed a bit nervous about the upcoming sale and move and expressed this anxiety in their own unique ways. The husband's tone became more heated as I continued with my initial consult.

"What can we do NOW?" the man demanded. "We need to be in the new apartment by next month."

The wife continued to ride shotgun without saying a word so I stopped the tour to answer the question for them both. I suggested that a great place to begin the process of sorting was in their library that housed hundreds of books. "You can decide which books will move with you and which books will be donated or given away," I said.

He agreed, she nodded, and we continued with the rest of the tour. At the end of our consultation, while reviewing my calendar for the first available start date, he said "Let's start Monday. We're ready." We had not even discussed how the process would actually work, how long it would take or the estimated cost. Due to our full schedule, the start date would need to be three weeks later. He was not happy, but agreed to the date. I promised to follow up the next day with a written proposal detailing the task list of issues we compiled, the potential launch date and the financial estimate.

The next day was Sunday, and I noticed that my mobile phone was buzzing relentlessly. I listened to the multiple messages, which became louder and angrier as each hour went by. It was the CEO who yelled into the mouthpiece, "My wife packed and lifted 50 heavy boxes...and because of you, she threw her back out! This is unbelievable – and all your fault!"

I returned the call and he immediately began to yell. I finally interrupted him and said, "I did not ask your wife to pack, lift and carry 50 heavy boxes of books!"

It turned out the CEO was so anxious about their impending move that he was the one who put her to work as not only a packer, but an actual mover.

The moral of the story is to take a breath and look at this process logically instead of just racing around, filling up boxes and then pulling muscles by lifting them. Most of us aren't in the kind of shape where we should be lifting 50-pound boxes. If you need help, ask for it or hire it. Don't allow emotions to run so wild that everyone is suddenly spinning their wheels to an unfortunate end.

Your Interior Assessment is Over. Now What?

We've come to the end of our indoor tour. At this point, you've compiled a task list of some of the issues you've noticed that will need to be addressed before your house is ready to go on the market. The list is typically longer than you would like, but this is not uncommon. Take a deep breath and let's move on.

The observations and recommendations are not typically issues that you were unaware of, but ones you were hoping would not be considered "issues." Together, we will review the most common items on the assessment list in future chapters and make sure that each is addressed.

It's time to discuss our next steps including the vendor estimates necessary for the work to be done.

Wait just a second!

We're not done. We still have to explore the outside, but before we do, let me remind you to detach emotionally. Again.

From this point on, we will stop referring to your house as your HOME.

We will now refer to your home as a HOUSE. A product. Your most valuable ASSET.

Let's make sure to present this asset to the buyer in a manner that reflects *value to them* from the moment they get out of the car and are on their way to the front door. (Not *your* front door because remember…you're moving).

As your mind begins to swim with the information about the changes that are necessary before you list, let's step outside.

Chapter Four

Exterior Assessment

It's impossible to find a Realtor today who doesn't drive home the importance of curb appeal. An attractive and well-presented exterior can mean the difference between a house sale and a house that sits on the market gathering dust. Sadly, you can have a house with a beautiful interior that is never seen due to the negative assumption from agents and buyers based on the exterior presentation. It follows that improving the visual appearance of the exterior of your structure and property is one of the best investments you can make as a seller.

According to the NAR, 63 percent of homebuyers will ask for a showing after viewing a house online. The first thing they will see – even in pictures – is the exterior of your house. Understand that a potential buyer has already taken a positive step in deciding to tour your house. They have viewed the listing online and are impressed enough to schedule a physical tour of the property. Be sure that what they see in person – what comes to life after looking at those photos -- is in keeping with the positive impression they formed when they viewed the listing online. If they see perfection in the way the exterior is maintained, they will assume perfection in the way that the interior is maintained. Five rusted bikes on the front porch? Not a good sign. This is why they call it curb appeal in the first place.

So, what defines curb disaster? Let's start with a roof that's missing shingles or is dingy or streaked. Is algae growing up there? Are there oversized trees that prevent you from seeing the front door? Can you read the house numbers or are they dark, dull or non-existent?

The minute I drive up to a house, I notice every aspect of the exterior façade and surrounding property. I am consciously trying to frame the exterior photo in my mind. You can do this, too. Step outside and cross the street. View the exterior of your house as a buyer will. Ask yourself the questions below and "score" your exterior in relation to the necessary visual perfection that buyers expect today. My first glance looks quickly at the following areas:

- What color is the house?
- What color are the shutters?
- What color is the front door?
- Is this color combination complimentary?
- Does the front door hardware match; Is it in good condition?
- Do I see any peeling paint?
- Do the shutters need painting?
- Is the window trim cracked?
- Is the siding in good condition?
- Is the stucco cracked?
- Is there outdoor lighting? Does it work?
- Do the iron railings need to be sanded and painted?
- Is the hardscape in good shape or missing stone and

chunks of mortar? Does it need to be power washed?

- Are any roof shingles loose or missing?
- Does the roof need to be power washed?
- Are the gutters overflowing with leaves?
- Are the windows void of cracked panes and clean?
- What is the condition, size and shape of landscaping (trees, plants and flowers)?
- Is the plant material blocking the front façade of the house?

Would **you** pay top dollar for **this** house? If not, let's move on. But, before we do...

A Quick Story: The Invasion of the Azaleas

I have before and after pictures of a colonial house where a couple lived for over 40 years and raised a lovely family. The kiddos were grown and it was time to downsize. When I stepped out of the car for the initial consultation, I stood in front of a two-story brick house feeling like I was in some kind of real estate horror movie called "The Invasion of the Azaleas."

The house itself was in pristine condition but was hidden behind a huge visual wall of azaleas. Those pink, red and white gigantic bushes – planted circa 1975 – had pretty much taken over almost every square inch of the front yard landscaping. They were everywhere! Blooming! Crowding! Over the years, they just matured ...and expanded...and exploded. I was screaming on the inside knowing that anyone who wasn't a horticulturist would give this curb appeal a zero in spite of the profusion of natural seasonal colors.

Of course, one person's flower horror story is another's…flowering nirvana.

The woman of the house greeted me with a warm smile, gazed at her front yard and said, "Isn't it beautiful? So many flowers. It's like a flower store." (The only problem: Buyers want a house and not a floral mart!) Perhaps there was a time when the owners actually had the advantage over the Attack of the Azaleas or as I call it, "the uni-bush," but the truth was it was time to have an honest talk with the seller and call a gardener about the overgrown landscaping.

Back to Your Buyer

Buyers expect a well-manicured exterior. Front and backyard areas are now considered "must-haves" and if they're well-maintained will prevent buyers from quickly returning to the car before they even make it to the front door.

Look beyond your own personal preference and taste and ask yourself: Does my home have the curb appeal to sell quickly and for top dollar?

One word about backyards: They aren't even called that anymore in some real estate markets; they're referred to as "outdoor retreats." Seriously? Many buyers want their yards to reflect what you'd expect at a five-star hotel. Gone are the days when the front and back grassy areas were just a little green patch of lawn or a place for the kids to play on a swing set. In 2019 and beyond, it's all about what's dubbed "indoor-outdoor living" or "bringing the indoors, outdoors"–even when it's five degrees below zero outside.

I knew if my azalea queen became a client, I would ask my landscaper to bring two trucks, rolls of fresh sod and a plan to create a new front garden as a reflection of the classic, beautiful and inviting house that was hidden from view. It's not hard to re-landscape a garden to sell or even wildly expensive. You will start with a plan that will include plant material in a style that compliments the house and locate the most cost effective place to purchase the plant material. The most common impediment to this course of action is typically the seller who resists change and is not willing to consider an alternative to their personal preference.

EXTERIOR OVERVIEW

The Front Façade

It's time to tour the outside and focus on the front exterior. I'll be looking at the visual condition of the structure, roof, chimney and gutters. The color of the paint, shutters and front door are also critical to our assessment. Does the house color scheme work together? The goal is to present visual perfection without breaking the bank for the seller. The great news is that front and back exteriors are often easily fixed with low cost, high impact solutions including easy DIY projects that the seller can complete.

A few first fixes when it comes to the front curb appeal:

Paint: Be honest. When is the last time you painted the outside of your house? If you can't even remember who the President was when a roller or brush hit your home, then that's a sign that you probably need to do it before putting the house on the market. Is the paint peeling? Is it faded from the sun in certain areas? Stained from tree leaves in others? Does your house look fresh and new? Or does it look a bit tired as the once-black paint on the wood is now a winter-weathered gray. One of the quickest and least disruptive (to everyday life) fixes that can help to make your house sell faster is a fresh coat of paint.

Roof: Is the roof missing shingles or streaked with green algae? This is not uncommon and does happen over time. Remember, this process is a visual one and very different than an actual roof inspection by a roofer or home inspector. They're the ones who will find the structural issues and the leaks.

Bricks And Mortar: Are the bricks in good shape or are they chipped, broken or missing? Many homeowners have replacement bricks in reserve that provide quick saves. If the mortar is loose, cracked or non-existent, it's time to think of replacing it to make the house look well maintained and deflect concerns from a buyer about possible structural damage.

Chimney: No chimney cap? Missing bricks or stone? Obvious cracks? Another item to put on the replace or repair list.

Shutters: I always take a close look at the shutters to make sure that they're not warped or missing any slats. Are the "S" clips secure or missing? I've made million-dollar homes look like model homes by purchasing and replacing older, rotted wooden shutters with inexpensive vinyl shutter replacements and new "S" hooks from Home Depot. You can, too.

Windows: Full window replacement is often beyond the budget of most home sellers and is almost never necessary to sell the house. This update is a major home improvement, typically costing over $10,000, depending on the total number of widows that will be replaced. To be clear, if not replaced, windows need to at least look clean with clear (not cloudy) glass, properly lock and open and close with ease. Replacing individual glass panes that appear cloudy or are cracked is a less expensive alternative than paying thousands for a full window replacement.The trim should be void of any cracks or any peeling. Skylights should be clean and properly sealed.

Aluminum Siding: Replacing aluminum siding is an easier fix than warped or rotten wooden shingles on the façade of a home. Is the siding in good condition without any dents, dings or peeling edges? Check your siding or home warranty to see if replacing pieces can be done quickly and at no cost. Is the siding all there, but dull, dirty and dusty from a hot, rainy summer or an especially snowy winter? Perhaps your siding just needs a quick, professional power wash to make it look new again.

Exterior Lighting/Outlets: A poorly lit or dark house exterior can look unappealing/scary/haunted (and a plethora of other buyer concerns), and many potential buyers work full-time and will be touring your home after daylight hours. No buyer wants to pull up to the house and not immediately see a well-lit path to the front door. Check the light fixture(s) just outside the front door. Are they old and rusted and need to be replaced? Or is it a hanging fixture? Does it provide adequate light? Does your home have two bigger outdoor lighting fixtures on either side of the attached garage... and that's it?

Exterior lighting is an art, and it's often helpful to take a quick car trip around the neighborhood at night to see who has done a great job with it.

Driveways: Assess large settlement cracks in the driveway to assure a buyer that the land that the house sits on is sound and safe. Remind yourself to remove weeds between driveway bricks and power wash if necessary. Think about limiting the number of cars in the driveway and plan to remove extra cars, strollers, bikes, campers and other objects "parked" there. Your driveway is no longer a storage spot.

Front Step: Is the landing welcoming and tidy or a place where the contents of the house spill out? One past project featured an old Christmas tree fully decorated and proudly displayed *all year around*. On another, the homeowner's collection of concrete decorative creatures created a virtual maze to the front door. Plan to clear it all out and replace with a simple planter or two.

Front Door: Ask yourself if the first impression visually and physically match up. If the handset is in bronze, polished brass or brushed nickel, the knocker, mail slot and kick plate should also be matched in bronze, polished brass or brushed nickel. Does the handset need to be replaced? Does it look skimpy or inadequate for a house at your price point? "Door jewelry" is critical to convey the impression of a well-designed and secure front door. Does your door need a fresh coat of paint? Remember, your door is one of the first things a buyer will see when they knock and wait to be let inside.

Landscaping: I know you have that great elm or pine tree in front of your house and that it was planted by dearly departed Uncle Walter. It is beautiful, but overgrown. It's now 30 years later. Is it blocking the entire front facade of your house from the street? It's time to think about scheduling a landscaping service to trim it back or remove it, entirely. There are times that I advise homeowners to actually remove an entire front garden bed that is visually overgrown and out of control and replace it with new plant material. While it is often an emotional decision for the seller, it is not for me. The question is simple: Does this front garden highlight the house? If not, what will you do to change it so that it does? Trees that are lifeless, leaning into or over the house or look like they're dying or half dead should be removed. This may be an expensive fix at $1,000 or more for large tree removal, but buyers may demand that it be done before closing. Be forewarned.

The Backyard

As we mentioned earlier, backyards are now playing a larger part of the American dream and sellers need to look carefully at the way that their backyard currently presents. To begin, stand outside the back door. What do you see? Where is your eye drawn? Is your yard fenced in? Is it in good shape? Does the gate open and close without issue? Are the garden areas edged and mulched? Is the landscaping well-manicured? Is there a gauntlet of items on the side of your house (from bikes to old statues) that are using that area as their final resting spot?

Buyers want a well-maintained fence, if you have one, and a gate that works. Now, walk into the yard and look back at the house. Are the screens torn or missing? Is that back-patio door warped? All of this will need to be addressed or repaired before your house goes on the market or you might leave money on the table.

A quick glance around the yard might reveal an old dog house that needs to go or a dog run that is no longer used. Is there an ancient swing set from when your children were young, except now they're 27 and the swing set is no longer up to code? Yes, you thought you needed that big, leaking, space-devouring hot tub, but you haven't used it since 1996. Is your door surrounded with decorative eyesores?

Don't try to convince yourself that the new buyers will want that dried out koi pond with the broken filtering system or might want to re-paint your ancient and rusted playground equipment. They won't; get rid of it. The same goes for whatever is leaning against your home out back from bikes to old lawn furniture. Going-going-gone.

The lawn needs to be green and in reasonably good shape, mowed and without any holes and ruts. If it doesn't look well-maintained and fresh out there, it's time to make a plan to make sure that it does.

Hardscape: Look at the stonework throughout the property; walls, patios, and built-in features like fireplaces, outdoor grills and fountains. Is the stonework and/or cement or brick in good visual and physical condition? Or, is it cracked, crumbling and missing stones, brick or mortar? Patio stones should be secured with no missing mortar or blue stone dust. Outdoor grills, kitchens and fire pits should be clean and functional.

Fences: Take a long, slow walk along your fence line to make sure that it is straight, secure and the wood isn't rotten, warped or contain evidence of a termite infestation. If you have a chain-link fence make sure that it's not rusted. All gates must easily open and close.

Decks: A deck is a wonderful selling point. Check to be sure that it's clean, structurally sound and the wood is free of rot and evidence of termites, the boards level and not warped.

Pools: If your house has a pool, you will need to look closely to be sure that there are no cracked or missing tiles and the filter and automatic pool cover are are in good working order. If you list your house for sale before the pool is opened for the season, you can display photos of the pool and pool deck in warmer weather. Make sure that all pool railings are secure and slides and diving boards present in good condition.

Many buyers with small children will be hesitant to purchase homes without a protective, locked fence around the pool. Pool safety fences start around $1,500 including installation and materials. Prices are based on how much fencing is needed, the height of the fence, the number of gates and the surface that it will be installed upon. Fences are legally required in some communities if a child under a certain age limit will reside in the house.

Guest House/Pool House/Shed/Playhouse: Outdoor structures that are on the property or convey as part of the sale should receive no less attention than the house and grounds. Guest houses should present with the same level of design as the main house. Appliances must be in working order, lighting checked, and floors in good shape.

Now that we've completed the exterior tour of the house and property, I will ask you again, Would **you** pay top dollar for **this** house? If the answer is still no -- or if you're not sure -- it's time to create the Plan of Attack.

Chapter Five

The Plan of Attack

Most sellers that I meet with are physically and emotionally exhausted by the end of our tour. They are done with me and my "expert opinion" and are ready to have their house and privacy back. I see their glazed look and know that it's time to wrap it up. They can't move from their chairs and are completely overwhelmed with the scope of the project ahead. Are you feeling this way, too? This is a normal reaction as you consider the task list we compiled.

WAIT! It's about to get worse.

The minute you hear my car door slam or you list the last issue: Total panic sets in. Your brain is screaming, "This is indeed happening! We are (gulp) moving! This is a lot of work! This will cost a lot of money! Why are we moving? Whose idea was this in the first place? And why didn't we fix that backdoor years ago?"

The questions are endless. When will I find time to pack? What will I bring with me? How can I find the right mover? Will I ever get this old place in shape? … Can I… How can I…How much…

Stop. Breathe. Focus.

The process will begin with the strategic organization that I call the Plan of Attack. It will end after the last box is unpacked in your gorgeous new home.

It isn't just possible. It's the goal and you are not alone because I'm about to plan that attack with you. As a home transition expert, I shoulder the large majority of the emotional and physical burden that you are facing. But, there is a cost associated with hiring an expert, so, you have a decision to make. Will you do it alone and become a do-it-yourself, independent contractor to save money *or* will you work with an expert that transitions families from one home to the next on a daily basis? One of the primary benefits of working with a transition expert is that they will utilize their own vetted and trusted vendors to schedule the work to be done and supervise the quality of the finished product, so you don't have to.

Or, you can locate, vet, hire and supervise your own vendors. Your choice.

The Launch Schedule and Scope of Work

The timeline that we develop to detail critical dates is typically coordinated with your Realtor who will refer to this to create a launch schedule for the house. **The most important date for our planning purposes? It's when we have agreed to have the house and property 100 percent ready for the professional photo shoot.** Other critical dates are the scheduled pricing tour with the agent's local office to establish the list price, the MLS list date, appointment only showings, open house(s) and a public broker open. However, the photo shoot is our D-DAY. Our project must be completed a day or two before the photo shoot. As an example, we have determined that the entire project will take three and a half weeks to finish. I look at the calendar and circle May 4, for the photo shoot. I will also circle the start date for home improvement projects, April 1, which ensures ample time for unexpected delays.

At this point, we are not considering the actual move date. For most sellers, you won't select a move date until you have a ratified contract on the house and an agreed upon closing date. If you are a seller who has bought a new house and decided on an actual move date, we will discuss a new set of questions: Do you plan to take all your household goods to the new house even if the current house does not have a ratified contract? Or, are you planning to leave some furniture behind to stage the current house? You might take everything with you because it makes the most sense to do this in one move to settle your family and minimize the disruption of the transition. If so, you might consider hiring a staging firm with a furniture inventory to stage the vacant house. The cost of staging needs to be discussed and will vary depending on which area of the country you live in. This service can range from several thousand dollars to $10,000, or more. It depends on the size of the home, the experience of the stager, quality of furnishings and the number of rooms in the home that you will stage.

SMART MOVE: Download one of the many blank calendars available online to use as a planning tool along with this book. Create a transition binder to contain this calendar of several months to enter key dates, notes, meetings, vendor estimates, receipts and other house and move related documents you will need access to over the course of the project.

To Stage or Not to Stage?

Some people believe you only need to stage the first floor of your home. That is NOT a **SMART MOVE.** What may happen is that the visual excitement built up on the main floor completely falls apart upstairs when you are faced with vacant or sparsely furnished rooms.

An emerging alternative for sellers is virtual home staging. The online listing of your house is beautifully painted and staged with designer furniture while the house itself remains vacant. This option is less expensive, but creates an issue for *many* buyers. They arrive at the house and are immediately disappointed that the walls aren't the color they saw online and the furniture doesn't match or even worse, the house is empty. You don't want buyers to think, "This is not what I want…and it would take me $200,000 to get to that look."

Personally, I am not a fan of virtual staging. I believe you would be better off financially in certain situations to leave the house clean and vacant. The emotional letdown is distracting and negative for potential buyers.

What Can I Afford to Do?
What Can't I Afford NOT to Do?

Sellers need to strategically schedule their task list, but first, we need to discuss the budget you will operate within to visually prepare, cosmetically update and stage your house.

Most sellers *do* look at the task list from a purely financial standpoint. They are firm with their budget and have decided on a number that is "fair" to prepare their house to sell. Let's say it's $20,000.

I'll ask, "Why did you pick this number?" I'll hear, "Because we think it's about right." This budget may or may not be realistic given the scope of work that needs to be done. You may need to reassess your budget. Don't be tempted to "dig your heels in" and decide to address only the low hanging fruit or what is easier or cheapest. Although it is tempting to do.

> **SMART MOVE:** DON'T CHERRY PICK THE LIST! Fight your basic instinct to save money and just grab for the easiest and least expensive home repairs. You might save time, money or hassle in the short-term, but you'll be taking your eye off the grand prize of a faster house sale at a price point you will agree to and be happy with in the long run.

You should prioritize the list by visual and physical impact. It's often a decision of "this" is more important than "that." Perhaps you won't be re-sodding the entire lawn afterall, but you will install beautiful new bushes in the front garden and fresh mulch.

When I work with a client, we look at a budget together and discuss the priorities and where they will get the most impact for their dollar. A typical conversation might go this way: "We need to paint the entire interior and agree that the lighting will be replaced in these three rooms. We will fix those broken blinds in room two but replace them in room three. We will re-carpet the basement and re-tile over the current tile in the laundry room. We will also schedule the power washing, window washing and a landscape clean up."

I'll then ask the client, "Tell me about your capabilities. What work can *you* do on the list?"

> **SMART MOVE:** Create a budget to prepare your current house and property for sale. This budget must be based on actual estimates for the work to be done. Do not base it on the arbitrary figure in your mind that you believe it should cost, is fair and can justify spending to address each issue. Utilize the budget to complete items that will create high visual and physical impact for the buyer.

If your budget is limited for the sale prep then don't worry. This doesn't necessarily have to be expensive as you'll see in the next chapter when we begin to stage the rooms. You can work within the confines of any budget to deliver a house that looks fresh, clean and organized for buyers.

Reach out to trusted tradespeople for several estimates. Call friends and relatives who may be willing to help you during the process to redirect money in the budget. Call in favors and prepare to barter your skills for use at a later date. It's worth it to ask for the help that you need now. You will have ample opportunity to return the favor once you are settled.

Working With A Pro

Do you need to hire a pro? The answer might be yes if your schedule is so busy that you can barely make it through the average day. Adding a major move to the mix doesn't just *sound* mind-boggling, it *is* mind-boggling. My clients are *already* overwhelmed with work, kids, travel and responsibility. The idea of meeting with painters to get an estimate sounds horrific to them. My clients simply don't have the time to make the move priority number one or the mental bandwidth to deal with sorting, purging and packing up their treasures without help.

Breathe. Inhale. Relax. The hard part is over when you hire a transition expert. It's an option if your budget allows. You no longer have to worry about finding a good landscaper or trustworthy painter because I keep my favorites on speed-dial as will the experts in your area. A good home transition expert will take responsibility for tracking all the details, so you don't have to do it. Exhale.

Dealing With the Trades

Let's say you're in charge. For some sellers, there is nothing more stressful than dealing with tradespeople who can be intimidating and move to the beat of their own drums. They can be late, unpredictable and may not complete the job they were hired for. The quick tips below will help you to be prepared:

- Ask friends and neighbors for vendor recommendations. Realize that some of your friends may not share this information and it doesn't help to beg. Move on quickly to another source. Check online sites like Angie's List, HomeAdvisor, Thumbtack, Porch.com and neighborhood Listservs, plus others that provide basic company information, pricing structure and customer reviews.

- Utilize your Realtor's contacts to source referrals for trades they trust and work with on a regular basis.

- Set an appointment for the initial estimate. If the vendor misses the appointment, is late or reschedules more than once -- finito! If you're having scheduling issues at this early stage, it will be an issue throughout the project.

- Get two estimates (at least) for each type of repair. The costs can vary wildly based on location and experience.

- Schedule vendor estimates within several days of each other to select the vendors you will work with and schedule the work.

- Make sure all estimates are dated and in writing. If the tradesperson only provides an on-the-spot verbal estimate -- red flag. Pass.

- Compare apples to apples. For example, you can get two carpeting estimates. One carpet estimate includes upgraded carpet pads, but the cost is $100 higher. The other estimate includes a basic pad for no additional cost. Paying the additional $100 is worth it if the subfloor is cement. Without a thicker pad, it will FEEL like you are walking on the actual cement. Remember: apples to apples.

- Sign a contract with each vendor that details the scope of work, cost and date of completion. Many of my clients add a clause stating that a reduction of final payment will result if the deadlines are not met. This provides a great incentive to finish the project on time.

SMART MOVE: Ask to see contractor's licenses for all vendors, plus Workman's Compensation insurance certificates. Don't just take their word for it.

What Is the Difference Between Licensed, Bonded and Insured?

When you're hiring a contractor or tradesperson, you will hear the words licensed, bonded and insured. Let's break it down.

- **Licensed** means that your contractor has a business license as either a general contractor or a specialty contractor. Specialty contractors offer specific skills such as plumbing, electrical or drywall installation. The contractor's license number is legally required to be displayed on any posted marketing material. Unlicensed contractors might be less expensive, but you have no recourse if their work is substandard or left incomplete.

- **Bonded** means your contractor has purchased bonds to prove their stability to consumers. A bond is a contract between the contractor, the property owner and the bonding company. It ensures that your contractor has the financial backing in case the project is not completed or up to the level of expectation stated in the contract.

- **Insured** refers to a requirement by Federal and State law to cover their business. Most have general liability insurance to cover any damage to the property or its employees injured while on the job.

The Roller Coaster Ride Continues

We've identified the timeline, task list, budget and vendors. Now, it's time to start packing up a lifetime of belongings.

To return to the roller coaster analogy, you're about to experience soaring highs (the closet is clean!) and stomach lurching lows (I can't believe we have this much stuff!).

It's time to move this project forward another step.

We're going to start sorting, organizing, and packing, which will create another low as you sift through dresser drawers that haven't seen the light of day in years. At the same time, your home will soon be filled with boxes, packing paper and rolls of tape, which makes it all too real (low, low, low). Plus, you just agreed to turn the property over to the agent in several weeks and strangers will soon be invading your personal space (lower). Perhaps your home will sell in a nanosecond (super high)…or it might take months (super low) or years (the lowest of the lows). I hate to be the bearer of bad news, but the emotional roller coaster will continue until you unpack that last box in your new residence. Expect it. Buckle up. Ride through it until the end.

There is no real way to prepare you emotionally or physically to tear your home apart room by room. However, if you can anticipate the highs and lows along the way, you'll be better able to deal with the fluctuations. The day your painter will move your furniture out of place to paint the house won't feel as destabilizing if you know this will happen on week two of the six weeks you have until D-Day, the photo shoot. The day you receive a lowball offer on the house won't feel as devastating if you expect a few of them and will make the day you receive an excellent offer even better.

Procrastination is Enemy Number One

One of my clients only had a few weeks to move from a large home in the suburbs into a smaller apartment in town as the next step in her life plan. Her prior life as a socialite meant that she owned multiples of ball gowns, shoes, hats, scarves and other accessories in her mini-mansion because there were rooms to spare. Now, she was faced with extreme downsizing and told me she felt paralyzed. "We need to start sorting today," I told her. "How about in a week?" she begged. "I have to wrap my mind around it. I just want to hide."

That's a common emotion when it comes to trying to sort your things and deciding what to keep for your new home. Downsizing is especially difficult as you will no longer have as much space to spread out. Decisions on what to pack and keep must be made with care. You're excited about the new home, but getting to that point seems quite far away. And it is. There are thousands of decisions you will need to make about your belongings along the way.

I'll hear: "There is so much work to do! I'll start tomorrow."

There is no tomorrow.

> **SMART MOVE:** Follow the advice of psychologists who told WebMD.com that just setting aside 15 minutes each day for irrational worries – really verbalizing them to get it out of your system -- helps you to refocus your battle plan. Remember, "This too shall pass."

You're at the top of the roller coaster knowing that in a few short clicks, you'll be rushing downward again. You will have to examine all of your 300,000 household goods to decide what stays, what goes and what might help others if you donate. Prepare yourself mentally to complete this process because in many ways, it *is* the most difficult part to get through and may produce frustration, tears and screams. Commit to accomplish this with determination and with little drama by continuing to follow the Plan of Attack.

It's time to Brace for Impact.

Chapter Six

Brace For Impact

We *refuse* to let go of our "things," even if we really don't want them or use them. What are we afraid will happen if we let go of these things? Blame it on the emotional ivy! We have purposely planted and cultivated this ivy to grow on our homes and throughout our lives. The vines attach and spread through our "things" to provide deep personal and emotional meaning to them. It will climb over any obstacle in its path making it difficult to control and remove. Our ivy takes years to mature and constructs the backdrop of our lives and represents the "things" we value. That's why we have trouble letting go!

You look at that owl lamp and think, "Work of art." Someone else looks at it and thinks, "Garage sale." To each his own. The truth is we do own many, many useless things. Remember, most households contain 300,000 items. Additionally, according to the New York Times magazine, one out of every ten Americans rent off-site storage to house these "things." Off-site storage is the fastest growing segment of the commercial real estate industry over the past four decades. The culprit: Stuff, stuff and more stuff.

Our stuff also produces a great amount of stress and expense when we try to pack, store or move it. Basically, you have four choices when it comes to every item in your current home:

- Pack it
- Sell it
- Donate it
- Dump it

Bottom line: We're all treasure hunters and I have a lifetime collection of things myself. I typically don't tell a client what to keep and what to dump, although I will, if asked. Ultimately, you are the decision maker and it's up to you to decide what to keep and what to let go. My job is to provide the critical financial information and methods of disposition you will need to know to make an educated decision regarding the *cost* of keeping each of your household goods.

Your Personal Footprint

One of the first **SMART MOVES** you will make is packing up your personal footprint -- the treasures, trophies, personal photos, collectibles and other personal items that make your house a home. You'll be amazed at how this simple baby step allows you to "see" the space in which you are living. But, this is easier said than done.

Removing your personal footprint is an emotional challenge and will visually reinforce the decision you have made to move. Many families maintain that they can't live without these mementos for even a week, but they can, and they will. Think of the fun you'll have finding the perfect place for these items in the new house.

Touch Everything You Own Once

Before we can stage your home to sell, we have to clear it out. At this point, we're going to proceed logically room-to-room and take EVERYTHING OUT to view it all clearly and in one space. This means that everything comes off the shelves, out of the drawers and cabinets and is flung from the closets. You will touch everything once while you decide the future of that object. Why? **Remember that you're staging your home to sell while packing for your move at the same time.** You will identify and put aside any of the items you need to stage your house and pack up the items you decide to keep, but don't need for the next few months.

A dining room table is a great place to spread out and create areas to logically group the "like" items you have collected throughout each room in the house. For example, all crystal (glassware, plates, figurines), china (formal sets of plates) silver (flatware, bowls, platters, serving dishes, coffee/tea sets, candlesticks,) decorative items (artificial floral arrangements, collections) and personal photos will be placed in groups on the dining room table or carefully on the floor. View all that you own in each category to make a decision about the ultimate disposition of the item.

Ask yourself: Which are my favorites? What do I use most? What are duplicates? What looks worn?

This is the easiest part of the process for many sellers and will move quickly. Most of us will keep our valuable crystal, china and silver, but perhaps not have room for each piece. Take the time to decide *now* what you will not keep. Remember that the more you keep, the more you will have to move or store, which will require spending more money.

> **SMART MOVE:** Use ScotchBlue 3M painter's tape and a black Sharpie to place a piece of tape on each item or pile to designate: PK for Pack, S for Sell, D for Dump and Donate.

This process is what I call Brace for Impact for a reason. It does create the largest *mess* you have ever dealt with in your home, but by viewing all that you own, you will make faster, better quality decisions. Here's a deeper look at how you will categorize each item:

PACK IT. You'll pack it properly and store it on or off-site for the ultimate move to the new house.

SELL IT. If you no longer want or need an item, it's possible that it can be sold or consigned. The question to ask yourself is: Where and how do I sell it? What is the net sale amount, and can I afford the time and effort?

DONATE IT. If items are in decent shape, pass it on and feel good that another person will value it as you have.

DUMP IT. No one will love it; it needs to go to the local dump.

If you PACK IT, then you will need to add it to your household inventory for your binder. You will number each packed box and detail the list of items or write a general description on each box. For design planning purposes, you may want to take a photo and measure the furniture and the rugs that you will place in storage. This information will prove invaluable for the actual placement in the new house and you will refer to it while unpacking to pinpoint the location of items that are packed. I'll cover more about inventory in a moment.

The Process Isn't Easy

How do you pack up a lifetime? Start by looking for storage places for your packed boxes. Usually this is a basement or an attic, which are the rooms that we deconstruct first in any move. The next stop is the first floor where you will view each of the main rooms methodically. Sort, decide, pack and remove the dump and donation items and place in another room or area for the moment. The bedrooms and bathrooms can be next followed by all of the other rooms in the house. The kitchen can be last, as your family is probably still living in the home.

If there is a closet in any room, you can begin there by removing everything from it. Sometimes this is a solo job. Ask yourself, "Can anyone really help me sort and make decisions in this room?" If the answer is no, make time to focus on the area yourself like a home office. Sorting medical, personal and family files, correspondence and financial documents takes time and must be done by you and **only** you.

By sorting each room in your home, you will touch everything in your house **once** and make a decision about its disposition. For the items you can't make a decision about just yet, put them to the side with a notation: TBD (to be determined). When you are better emotionally equipped to deal with those items, you will return to the box. As you move forward with this process, give yourself permission to let it go and donate to charitable organizations, family, friends and neighbors. As the pressure on you continues to increase and the schedule tightens, your ability to make carefully thought-out decisions will be affected.

At this point in the process, the entire house looks destroyed.

Perfect! You are making progress by creating these large, organized piles that are growing with each decision you make. All the bar tools and cocktail napkins are in a little lump by the couch and memorabilia near the fireplace. This visual chaos is representative of your emotional roller coaster on its downward run and to feel discouraged is common, normal and expected. It's difficult to see the progress you have already made. But, take heart. You ARE making progress.

This phase of the project is long, tiring and definitely not a "finger-snapping event." It may take you several days or weeks, depending on the size of your home and the number of things that you own and need to sort. By taking the time to carefully consider the ultimate disposition of each item now, you will save both time and money later, by not packing it, paying to store it or moving it to the new house.

To remain on track, remember the sequence for each room: Empty (by taking everything out of drawers, closets, tables), evaluate (keep, donate, sell, dump) and execute (place in the correct action pile or box). It's tedious, but you will find it will get easier for you as you move through the house and your emotions take a backseat: You will simply force yourself to complete the task. Take frequent 10-to 15-minute breaks throughout each day, to ensure that you are physically able and mentally focused to make good quality decisions.

If you're part of a family unit that's moving, then it's important (for peace and sanity) to "stay in your own lane" when it involves sorting and packing. If you sort and pack your husband's or wife's home office and things that they need cannot be immediately located, they are bound to be upset. You would be, too.

Ask the chef in the family to sort and pack the kitchen. Make the best use of your time by sticking with your particular area of expertise. Divide and conquer, if possible. Explain the process to the older children in the family who can then be responsible for the sorting of their own rooms. Even the youngest child can take part in this process. You are providing them with the emotional "tools" to manage their own anxiety caused by the disruption to their daily routine. Give them each a small box, a roll of blue tape, a Sharpie and a piece of paper to create their own inventory list for you to include in the master inventory list. Some of these lists are not even legible and the descriptions hilarious while providing you with a much needed moment of levity.

Most older kids will appreciate being given this level of trust. You might tell them, "I won't let anybody touch your things, but I am here to help you to make decisions about them if you need me." Ten minutes later, they have moved on to the next activity and you will sort and pack the room yourself.

Children of the appropriate age understand the concept of charity when it's explained to them in simple terms, and most accept this life lesson easily and delight in filling a box with their old toys to donate. You may explain, "This is your chance to share toys and clothes with other kids who don't have as many toys and clothes as you do." It's always touching when the child fills a bigger box for others than he or she does for themselves.

After a few short days of packing using this sorting system, something funny happens: You're suddenly feeling more organized and in control of this process as semi-empty rooms begin to emerge. In fact, each room in your current home looks cleaner and larger. The roller coaster is approaching the top of another loop. You can do this! You are starting to emotionally disconnect and get more confident in making the tough decisions.

Get Emotional

Try hard to keep your emotions in check during this brutal process. Many sellers tell me that they're actually afraid to dig into their lifelong collection of things.

"Scared of what?" I'll ask them.

Most reply that they will regret getting rid of something that someday they might want or need. Based on my experience, the truth is "out of sight, out of mind." Moving into a new home is a perfect time to replace towels, blankets and furniture, even if it takes time to purchase what you want or need. Remember that the pain of giving away, selling, and tossing is like pulling off a Band-Aid. Once you feel the initial sting, you'll never feel the pain again. Only the memory of the pain remains.

This process causes tremendous anxiety for many sellers. The pressure of a timeline to sort out your life is constant. Once you begin the process, you have to continue until it's finished and stopping in the middle of the process is not an option. The possibility to "act out" is there and we all handle the stress of this process differently.

One of my clients is a CEO and her company ranks near the top of her niche industry. I truly admire her as she's a superhero. She had just purchased a much larger home and needed to pack up a rental house that the family had been living in for the last two years. At one point during the sorting and packing process, she looked up at me with tears in her eyes and a trembling bottom lip and said, "Could you excuse me for just a minute?" She raced to her bedroom to cry her poor, stressed and emotional heart out. Yes, she could run an international business, but she fell apart deciding which art projects her kids had created should be keepers. She was pulling at the tendrils of her emotional ivy each time she tried to make a decision. "My whole world feels like it's upside down," she said, staring at years of school artwork in a pile on the floor. This pile was too overwhelming to sort at that moment. She was late to an important work meeting with a client and did not have the ability to deal with this particular "pile." I truly felt her pain.

In general, we do not deal well with physical and emotional change and disruption to our daily lives. We're creatures of habit and rely on our routines to keep us centered and balanced. You may have to dig deep to find the emotional strength to sort through the inventory of your life, but, by doing so now, you will keep only the most treasured and useful things as you move on to the next house.

The Exquisite Guilt of Not Wanting Our Parents' Things

It's a fact: Baby Boomers are growing older and downsizing now that their children are in college or have left the nest. At the same time, their parents are in their 70s to 90s and perhaps in long-term care facilities or smaller living quarters. As Boomers grow older, one of the things that they have in common is that they don't always want their parents' possessions. That Lenox wedding china that your mother promised you all those years ago? Don't expect a fight with siblings over who is going to "get it." No one wants it.

These heirlooms do require a potentially difficult, emotionally charged conversation with older parents whose adult children want nothing more than the family photos, which they've already moved to a flash drive. "Mom was so upset that I didn't want her large crystal collection, but where would I put it in our new 2,500 square foot condo?" a client asked me.

Remember that Boomers are the post-World War II adults who believe that amassing fine possessions is a marker of success in life. Times have changed. We are overwhelmed with our own "things" and may crave a simpler lifestyle and home that is more organized and minimalistic in design.

What can you do if you have no place for your parents' items?

The only solution is to have an honest conversation with your parents about what you would love to keep and mutually decide what should happen to the rest of their treasures including auction, eBay, resale stores and donations. Remind your parents that the things you treasure are the family photo albums, special books, pieces of art and other one-of-a-kind family mementos. Of course, the other option is to store the goods, which is why the $32.7 billion storage business is projected to grow at 3.5 percent annually over the next five years, according to Square Foot Storage Beat. Storage is often just a way to delay making difficult emotional decisions.

Take photos of the furniture that defined your youth that you have decided to donate. The photo will remind you of the piece without having to deal with the physical reality and the financial cost of storage. Resist the urge to delay the inevitable disposition decisions and rent a storage unit that costs you money, perhaps for years. Focus on your memories and donate the furniture and other collectibles to families that will build new memories with each piece.

Like many of you who are struggling with how to deal sensitively with this topic, I wrote a letter to my own 88-year-old mother.

A Letter to Mom

Dear Mother:

I am so sorry! I don't want your STUFF and the guilt is killing me!

Yes, we have actually had this conversation, several times lately, in my mind. In reality, I can't bear to tell you the truth -- that I not only don't want YOUR stuff, but I don't want Grandma's stuff either! UGH. What is wrong with me?

Some of my earliest happy memories are of the many holidays at Grandma's house when the dining table was dressed in her best linens, china and crystal. The kids felt so grown-up drinking apple juice in heavy crystal wine glasses at the "adult" table and grabbing handfuls of peanuts in the shiny sterling silver bowls.

Oh, to be grown up. I wish I knew then that all rites of passage were not as clear-cut and easily travelled.

When Grandma died, you absorbed all of her beautiful "things" without question to continue the traditions you both held sacred. You never questioned whether you wanted them or needed them. You just took them all and continued to honor her each time we used her beautiful things. You effortlessly took over the holiday meals and the multi-day preparation of the house to accommodate our relatives from far and wide. Nothing but the best for our guests! Out came the "good" china, crystal and silver. It was lovingly cleaned and polished, the linen pressed, and napkins placed in sterling silver rings. Like Grandma, the elegance of the day appeared like magic to us. I didn't realize how much time it took to prepare. I can't believe that you actually did that. How did you find the time?

I am so happy that you and Dad have decided to downsize. It's the right decision at the right time for you both. Lately though, I dread each phone call we have as the move date gets closer. You seem to be getting more emotional about leaving the house where you raised our family and desperate to find a good "home" for the family "treasures," each with its own story. You continue to gently pressure me to make a date to come over to choose the things that you are SURE that I will want for my own house and kids.

Mom, the truth that I can't bear to tell you is that I don't WANT to choose any furniture, artwork, Oriental rugs and gee-gaws that have been in our family for years. I feel ashamed to say that I have no use for your and Grandma's wedding china carefully preserved in soft felt-lined bags. I don't even use my OWN wedding china, it's in the attic! But I can't tell you that. I feel so guilty for even thinking that. So, I don't. I chicken out each time. I listen and agree that I need to make time to come over. Soon. And I will. Soon.

You know that we live in a newly built Craftsman style home with soft gray walls and white linen drapes. My rugs are all a sisal Berber blend and the furniture is white with gray accents. The overall design is minimalist, transitional, and soothing to me and my busy family. How do I explain to you that I actually LIKE the furniture I have and do not WANT the dark mahogany, cherry and walnut furniture that both you and Grandma have used in your homes? I don't WANT the dark Oriental rugs, no matter how unique they are and where they came from. I don't have time to entertain using all of my "good" china, crystal and silver. I actually LOVE my plain, white everyday china from Crate & Barrel, and I use it even when I set the table for "company."

I don't WANT to wash see-through bone china by hand. My white cotton napkins are from HomeGoods and go right into the washer after dinner. I don't WANT to use the Belgian linen napkins and doilies that the old ladies lost their eyesight creating. My crystal wine glasses and barware are simple and serviceable. No, they are not the beautiful Waterford set I got from Aunt Marge for our wedding. Those, too, are collecting dust in the attic. I have no use for the tableful of sterling silver flatware, serving dishes and platters that you used to entertain. And aside from the family holiday dinners I now understand I will be hosting, I can't possibly use all the formal linen tablecloths and napkins you have set aside for me.

I don't actually say this to you. I feel so guilty. I tell you that I will come over. Soon.

I know that you would not understand that my generation lives more simply. I live more simply and do not want to fill my life with more THINGS, even if it will make you happy. What will I actually DO with it all? I know that I won't use it and have no room to store it. I can barely keep up with the stuff that MY family accumulates. I know that you will never sell our family treasures. Right now, they are not worth much, as no one else wants them either. You know this. That is why you are counting on me to take them, store them and keep them safe for the next generation. Because if I didn't take them what would you do with it all? So, we will have this conversation and I will tell you how I feel. The next time you call and ask me about it. I will. Probably. Maybe.

I have been wondering if there is another way to honor you and Grandma and our family history without taking a complete house full of "treasures" that I don't want and have no room for. Can we take photos of them for posterity and donate them to a family that would love them and use them as we have through the years? Would you ever agree to that? Maybe you NEED to complete this rite of passage with me as your mother did with you by entrusting the next generation to honor the past by safeguarding its "treasures." If that is the case, I guess I will have to come over and choose the things that you want me to have. I am not sure what I will do with all of it, but if it makes you happy... I guess I will do it for you. And Grandma. But I am going to have this conversation with you the next time you call. There has got to be another way. We will discuss it. Definitely. Probably. Maybe.

With all my love,

Caroline

Can't Let It Go?

A client came to me and said that she "just could not" give up her parents' French country bedroom set, which has been stored for over five years. UGH. The monthly cost! "Will you use it in your new home?" I asked. She shook her head. "I really hate that style and I can't even imagine using it in a guest room, but I could never get rid of it because they loved it." My advice is to take a picture of the beloved family item and then donate it. Think of who you may be helping if you just let it go.

Donating is magical. Instead of paying to store an item you do not use or truly want, you pass it on to someone who will want it, use it and truly value it. Decide and then let it go. You don't want to be that person who says, "I don't even know what's in my storage unit."

I have clients who spend more than $1,000 a month renting large, climate-controlled storage units, but I ask, "Is it really worth it?" If the storage unit is filled with furniture that you no longer want and do not *ever* plan to use, why delay the decision to donate it? Think carefully and look at the monthly costs for storage. Is it worth it to you to continue to pay for the privilege of holding onto these "things?"

The self-storage industry is a great option for those who consider it temporary and are fully aware of the ever-rising cost of storage facilities (see sidebar below). Once you utilize this option, it may be difficult to reverse it. Rates designed to make short-term storage an emotionally and financially attractive option will often increase on a regular schedule. Do your homework. Do you want to avoid the financial mistake of "out of sight, out of mind" and pay the monthly cost for years to avoid having to deal with "it?"

I learned the lesson myself while getting divorced years ago. The kids and I had to downsize to a smaller rental home from the much larger marital home. It was critical for me to sort, organize and pack *only* the items that we truly valued and needed for our next home to avoid the cost of monthly storage for items that we wanted, but didn't have the space in our new rental to keep. We had to let go and we did. The truth is that the large majority of valuable items we owned came from my husband's mother and extended family. I didn't define myself by owning these things and the kids were too young to understand, so when my ex-husband reclaimed the antique furniture, Herend china, Georgian silver, Baccarat crystal, paintings, and many other high-value items we owned, I was at peace. I knew I would be able to create a beautiful home again- and I did-at a different price point and in a different style.

I am reminded of one seller, in particular, who learned this lesson the hard way.

She had a beautiful old colonial home in Chevy Chase, Maryland, a tony suburb of Washington, D.C. The house was filled with religious "treasures," her term for the items that she valued and lovingly displayed on almost every surface in the home. The agent offered this client a consultation with me at no cost to her, to discuss what might need to be done to prepare the house to sell and move. She was not interested in meeting with me at that time and was eager to put the house on the market. The house was listed on the MLS for six months without a single written offer. At this point, she was truly perplexed why the house had not sold yet and agreed to meet with me. A contract was signed and we began to work together. During the sorting and packing portion of the project, she became visibly discouraged by the amount of "things" she owned, sat down and said, "I can't see the forest for the trees." Neither could the buyer.

Over the course of the project, the team fell in love with this sweet woman who baked cookies to share and greeted us each morning perfectly coiffed and dressed. When I gently handed her the first roll of blue painter's tape and a black Sharpie, she looked a little rattled. Knowing what needed to be done, she began to fill her keep box and her donate box. She laughed that she had new "jewelry" -- her roll of painter's tape sat on her wrist along with her collection of David Yurman cable bracelets. Within 30 days, the house had a ratified contract.

Ready to Let It Go?

It's time to purge what you no longer want or need.

How do you know the difference between what to donate and what to dump? Do this with your head, not your heart. Be cutthroat about it. Donations should include gently worn clothing, furniture, coats, blankets, toys and books, among many other categories. What people do not want is your kids' school artwork, sculptures, paintings and other personalized items. Toss clothing that is too worn, stained or torn and generally beyond repair. These items are not of value to others.

There are many clients who are unsure where to donate their household goods beyond AMVETS or the Salvation Army. There are many different charitable organizations that will welcome your gently used household goods including: Dress For Success, local shelters for women and children, churches, community centers, fire houses, police stations and schools.

My Favorite Places to Donate and What They Need

- The Beethoven Foundation (musical equipment)
- Big Brothers Big Sisters Foundations (clothing, bedding, toys, games)
- Goodwill (clothing, furniture, toys)
- Habitat for Humanity; Habitat for Humanity ReStore (furniture, building materials, clothing, office supplies)
- Pianos for Education (pianos)
- Random Acts of Flowers (floral vases)
- Resale Charities (clothing)
- Ronald McDonald House (movies, toys, sports equipment, books)
- Salvation Army (housewares, decorative items, clothing, baby items, pool tables)
- Toys for Tots (unopened and boxed stuffed animals, toys)

A client once mentioned to me that she felt great satisfaction donating the work suits she no longer wore to Dress For Success. She felt good about the donation because she knew that she was providing an outfit that women would wear to life-changing job interviews. Check out the charities in your local area and find out what they need.

The Right Storage Facility

If you're still committed to those items and choose to store furniture and packed boxes in a long- or short-term storage facility, then you need to understand the differences between them to weigh the options and cost. I always recommend a climate-controlled storage unit to protect your goods against cracking, splitting, warping, yellowing, corrosion, rust, mildew, mold and bacteria. A typical short-term storage facility will allow you 24-hour access to your unit. **You can certainly use a short-term one for longer term storage, and some sellers do, but be aware of and willing to pay the rising cost of the unit over time.**

Longer term storage offered by many moving companies may be a preferable and lower cost option to store household goods that you will not need ready access to. Warehouse storage will typically use large wooden pre-made crates of varying size to hold your boxes and wrapped furniture. These seven by seven foot crates, for example, are packed and loaded onto pallets or "skids" in horizontal rows and stored on multiple levels of shelving to double or triple the capacity of the storage warehouse. Access to palletized storage is not impossible, but difficult to arrange and may incur additional fees to access. PODS are yet another alternative for sellers who would prefer the convenience of having the "storage" delivered directly to their house, filled and magically disappear. Specialty storage is often necessary to store the following: pianos, contents of wine cellars, valuable artwork and sculpture. These experts will ensure proper packing, transport and storage.

- Doctor Offices (magazines)
- Libraries (books)
- Local Hospitals and Children's Centers (DVDs, CDs, holiday decor, desks, book shelves)
- Local Schools (books, desk supplies)
- Local Shelters (blankets, coats, clothing)
- Local Thrift Stores (clothing)
- Veterinarian Offices (towels and blankets for pets)
- Women's Shelters (work clothing, children's clothing, books, baby clothes)

Additional Storage Tips:

- Research local storage options because cost and service vary widely.
- Compare client reviews on Angie's List, Yelp and Google, among other sites.
- Check the Better Business Bureau (BBB) for registered consumer complaints.
- Schedule a site visit to see the facility and meet the on-site manager. Select a unit that is clean, safe, well lit, accessible and regularly pest-controlled.
- Contact two local moving companies to discuss long-term warehouse storage capability and monthly cost per crate.
- Read the fine print in a storage contract and clarify automatic price increases over the course of the contract.

Whichever option you decide will best fit your storage needs, consider this solution to be short-term. Beware of "free" one-month specials and financially attractive incentives and understand what "free" will cost you over time. For example, sellers may agree to secure the storage unit with a credit card. They appreciate the "convenience" of the monthly autopay option. What they may NOT realize at the time, is the initial $99 a month will increase at preset intervals over the course of your contract. Quickly, the $99 per month becomes $150 per month.

Appraisals

Perhaps your items don't need to be boxed or stored. They can be sold or auctioned. While guiding the transition of thousands of families through the years, I recall many examples of valuable items found in attics, basements and storage rooms. One of my favorite stories involves a client who lived in his very large house for over 40 years and had recently made the decision to downsize.

While sorting his attic, we identified several different and unique collections gathered at different times throughout his life. When I told him that the collections were now displayed and ready for him to make decisions, he laughed and instructed me to "donate it all." Unconvinced this was the correct course of action, I immediately suggested that I contact a certified appraiser I frequently work with to confirm that the "collections" held nothing of "true" value and should be donated to the appropriate charitable organization. As it happens, the ugly, wooden, misshapen bowl we uncovered was actually a rare Inuit artifact! Needless to say, the $17,000 check he received from the sale of it in a specialty online auction was a welcome surprise.

The estate of a local, well-known Washington, D.C. matriarch whose family business was nationally recognized, required the expertise of *several* different certified appraisers to examine the unique collections and one-of-a-kind items throughout the house. These collections needed to be valued and sold before the house could be put on the market. Imagine those 600 English biscuit tins that were each carefully examined, priced and sold in an international auction for a huge sum. Who knew? So, it does happen, but my advice is to temper your hopes because for every hidden Picasso in the attic there is a paint-by-numbers version right next to it.

Sellers that are downsizing believe that they can sell almost everything they no longer want or need from their larger home. In theory, this is true. In reality, I have found it harder to do. You will need to research value, contract and pay an expert who will do the online legwork including tracking the sale and arranging for delivery. This typically means that you are storing the items until they are sold. This process does not guarantee a successful sale and may take weeks or months to complete. Think it through. More often than not, I hear from sellers that the sales price net of commission and the labor costs associated with delivering the item(s) is not worth the money and the hassle to sell it. In retrospect, you may wish that you had donated it. (See the Appendix of this book for how to contact a local appraiser).

What if you believe that you *do* own an item that could be valuable? If you are still not sure how to value an item, or to establish if there actually *is* value, schedule an appointment with a local certified appraiser who will quickly let you know and provide you with the guidance on how to sell it and the expected net price you *may* receive.

Several years ago, a client of mine owned a gorgeous grand piano that was appraised for a high dollar amount but that she *knew* wouldn't fit into her new home. She researched the current value of this piano and posted a picture and detailed description on Pianomart. com. Several weeks passed and she became frustrated with a lack of interest. So, unable to wait any longer to sell it, she decided to donate this beautiful and valuable piano to her daughter's high school. The school was thrilled to have it to replace the piano of lesser quality that they were currently using. Valuable, larger household items such as pool tables and home gyms often find a new home at police and fire stations or community centers. Furniture, in general, is often welcome at local parish halls or retirement homes. Be mindful of what you are donating and which organization will benefit the most from receiving those items.

Estate sales are a widely used vehicle to sell your household goods. Sellers often believe that they will make a " killing" by having an estate sale, and some actually do. The key is to keep in mind the net sales figures that will go to YOU. The commision to use a professional service will typically cost between 30 to 40 percent of the total sale. They may also need to host the sale at your home and the timing may conflict with your closing date and preparation for the move. Remember that the purpose of the sorting and packing process is to *remove* the items you no longer wish to keep, not store them for a sale at a later date. For this reason, an auction house that will store your items pre-sale may be a preferable option. If the items are not sold, the auction house will donate them to local charity.

A Quick Story: Lost and Found

Mr. A and Mr. G were sophisticated city dwellers who went out to the "country" (20 minutes north of Washington, D.C.) on a bright and sunny Saturday afternoon and gave into a whim. They purchased the main house on a former estate that was now surrounded by newly built homes. Shortly after selling their city condo and moving into the new house, it became clear to them that "country" living really wasn't their style. Three years later (after barely using the "country" house), they decided to put it on the market, so it was off to the "country" for me and my team. I was hired to design the house to sell and pack and store the items that would not be used to stage the house.

"Pack up everything and put it into storage," they instructed.

As usual, I took everything in every room out of drawers and closets to organize it in groups to be packed and inventoried. Lo and behold, I found: a loaded gun, sex toys, a Rolex watch and a big wad of cash on the bedside table. The house was full of surprises. After several days of packing, I received a panicked call from the clients. "Where are our file cabinet boxes?" they cried. To which I replied, "I already sent them to the short-term storage unit."

"I forgot to take out a bank bag that contains $20,000 in petty cash!" one wailed.

OOPS!

The crew that packed the file cabinets never saw a bank bag in the file drawer. After discussing with the owners the exact location of the bank bag, which cabinet and which drawer, I immediately drove to the storage facility to meet the anxious sellers and locate the missing bag. Itemized inventory in hand, I calmly replied -- "It's in box 43." And it was exactly in that box. A few minutes later, cash in hand, my very relieved sellers were on their way back to the big city. Who knew?

One of my all-time favorite seller stories involved the family of a mother in her eighties who had recently passed on. She left her home to her four adult children, all of whom lived locally. They had decided to sell the house immediately, so that they could each move on with their lives. Near the start of the project, I received a phone call from the oldest daughter. "My Mom always wore my Dad's wedding ring around her neck on a chain," she said. "The sad thing is that Mom lost the chain and the ring. In fact, no one has seen either for the last 15 years. It's lost, but just maybe you'll find it."

This wasn't the only family heirloom that was missing. A few days later, a second daughter called to let me know that her parents' wedding album was also missing, "We haven't seen it in decades and have no idea where she might have put it," the daughter told me.

"I will take personal responsibility to find both," I told her, knowing that I'd be going through her mother's possessions with a keen eye at finding these "lost" things. If these items were still in the house, I was sure that I would find them.

Sometimes, I just have to "play" detective. People often place something in a special spot for "safe keeping," but then forget where they put it. One day during the first week of the project, I was emptying Mom's large mahogany secretary in the master bedroom. Like most secretaries, it had many small drawers just above the drop-down desk used for writing letters. On my quest to find the ring, I thought this might be a likely hiding spot. While reaching my hand into the upper recesses of the left-hand, tiny drawer, I felt a tissue and gently pulled it out.

Inside was the husband's wedding ring hanging on the gold chain. A few days later while clearing out a closet in the family room, I found the wedding album. What a beautiful bride and groom!

Those are the good days.

The Local Dump

Is it truly *finito*? It's one thing to donate all those black skirts that are out of date and style. It's quite another to get rid of old building materials that are NOT moving with you…and no buyer wants them. How do you get rid of it once and for all?

The first step is to locate junk haulers in your area. Research these services the way you would any other vendor and ask for recommendations, check reviews and company websites to compare services and pricing information. Ask about the size of their trucks, so you'll know if your items will fit. My preferred hauling service has trucks that can hold up to roughly 10 living room sofas (truck bed size: 11' x 8' x 5'), but not all services have trucks this large. Next, understand pricing structure as it relates to truck size and partial loads. Be clear about the cost of gas, labor, and multiple stops. Are they included in the base price or do they require an additional fee?

Inquire about minimums in cost. A company may not be interested in picking up that one large statue in your yard unless you pay the minimum price regardless of its size or how long it will take to remove. Consider your options carefully and create an apples-to-apples analysis to make the most cost-effective decision for your items. Additionally, many of these companies now offer to pick up both donations and dump items at the same time and in the same truck. This makes the process easier for you. The truck then unloads the donations in a large warehouse where representatives from local charities actually come to pick up the donations. Easy.

PACKING 101

Pre-Move, In-Home Storing Strategy

Remember how you sorted your basement and attic first? We did this in order for you to create space for the boxes that you will now pack. Deep clean these empty spaces now as they will become valuable as you fill them with what you intend to keep on-site while your house is on the market.

Yes, it's time to pack it all up.

Packing Materials

Purchasing the correct packing materials is critical to ensure the proper packing of each item. Knowing exactly what to purchase, and in what quantity, stumps most sellers. One of the least expensive outlets to purchase packing materials is Home Depot. You can also order your supplies online from Homedepot.com and they will arrive at your door. Avoid buying them in bulk at storage facilities where they are conveniently laid out and accessible, but more expensive due to their internal markup (50 percent markup is common). A professional mover typically *doubles* the cost of all materials; however, sellers justify the cost of this convenience to avoid the heavy lifting and guesswork involved in the type and quantity of packing materials needed over the course of the move.

The trouble is few of us know exactly how many boxes and how much tape we will need at the beginning of the packing process, but no worries. You can always send someone on another Home Depot run …or two…or five.

Don't forget that you will also need 3M ScotchBlue 1" painter's tape to place on your furniture and other items to be packed and black Sharpies to indicate the ultimate destination for each item. I've had sellers congratulate themselves for creating complicated color-coding systems to identify the destination for their furniture and boxes, and this system confuses everyone but the seller that created it. To prevent the confusion and misplacement that always ensues, stick with these simple tools of the blue tape and the Sharpie. The blue painter's tape is safe to use on any surface except gold leaf on lamps and frames, suede and leather. Once packed, the blue tape is an inexpensive visual tool that is placed on the top of wrapped furniture for the actual move to quickly determine placement in the new house.

Supplies You Will Need:

Confused about exactly what you will need to pack? Refer to this checklist or take a picture of it with your phone before you hit the Depot:

- Black Sharpies
- 3M ScotchBlue 2090 Safe-Release Crepe Paper Multi-Surface Painters Masking Tape in Tensile Strength. One-inch tape sold in bulk packs of nine rolls.
- 33 Gallon Black Trash Bags
- 33 Gallon Black Contractors Bags
- 33 Gallon Clear Trash Bags
- Bubble Wrap in Smaller and Larger bubbles, 175 or 300 ft. rolls
- Packing Paper or Unprinted Newsprint Sheets 20"x 30"/600 per bundle
- Paper Tape-NOT plastic tape
- Acid-Free Art Paper

- Small Boxes (16" x 12" x 12"), Medium Boxes (18" x 16" x 18"), Large Boxes (24" x 18" x 18"), Tall Wardrobe Boxes, Short Wardrobe Boxes, Dish Pack Boxes.

How Many Boxes and What Type

Dish pack boxes will include corrugated carton inserts with double-wall construction suited for breakables (china, dishes, crystal and glassware). There needs to be small boxes for books and other breakables, medium boxes for heavy items including larger books and other media, large utility boxes for pots, pans, toys and non-perishable food and small appliances. You will also need extra-large boxes for bulky, but light-weight items such as linens, towels, pillows or lampshades.

You'll also need wardrobe boxes with a metal hanger bar for your hanging clothes, so you can transfer them neatly to your new closet with minimal effort. And don't forget picture boxes to transport artwork, family portraits and framed posters. The number of boxes will depend on the size of the home and the contents within. I'm often asked how many boxes does the average move require?

Here's a quick starter's guide:
- Buy 25 small boxes for books and small decorative items that are fragile and cannot be overpacked
- Buy 25 medium boxes for generic items
- Buy 20 large boxes for bedding, towels and sports equipment
- Buy five dish packs for heavy kitchen items including everyday dishes

Inventory

A moving inventory is easier to create now due to more advanced and widely available Internet programs, apps and technology. Create an Excel spreadsheet or use a moving app to list each piece of furniture and each packed box. This inventory can also be printed and placed in your transition binder. There will be no time during this move to wonder, "Where are the kitchen utensils?" Grab your phone, laptop or transition binder to confirm that "Box 49" is filled with kitchen utensils and located in the basement storage room. You don't have to get *fancy* with this inventory, but keep it on hand and refer to it when needed. Use the black Sharpie to write specific room and content information on the top and sides of each box such as: DINING ROOM-WHITE DISHES, CRYSTAL SERVING BOWLS, BLUE WEDDING CHINA.

You need to identify valuable and important items that will ultimately go in your car to the new house. Label those boxes HAND CARRY. They might include: artwork, passports, prescriptions, sculpture, money, jewelry and important documents. These things are irreplaceable to you. Protect yourself and your treasures by packing them yourself and removing them from the house BEFORE anyone you don't know and trust enters your house. Keep them locked in the car until it is safe to move them into the new home. Invest in a safe deposit box at your local bank branch for smaller, more valuable items.

Prevent an issue by removing the temptation.

Last Word: Ahem, We Still Live Here

Breathe. Inhale. Exhale. You've sorted, packed and stored. For many of us, living in the house through this process is a given. You will remain in the house until the day that you are scheduled to move. The good news is that by sorting the entire house, you have created room to store the everyday things that you will need to use until the day you move out.

Just when you thought you could take a break; the tradespeople arrive to begin the work that you have contracted them to do. Be prepared to add to the task list you created and agreed to at the start of the process. The spaces you cleared out and cleaned may have revealed repairs necessary that were not seen during the initial consultation. These areas often include: closets that need to be painted, trim touched up, pinhole leaks that need to be fixed and rotting wood to be replaced, among other things. This is common for sellers during this process and needs to be expected. The actual wear and tear on the house over the years is now obvious.

And emotionally? What's left in your house feels strange to you, impersonal and odd in a way that you can't put your finger on. If this is the case, you have done your job correctly and removed your personal footprint to allow a potential buyer to see the actual "bricks and mortar" of the house that they are potentially buying. (The funny thing is the house is so clean and minimalistic that many clients say to me, "I wish I would have lived this way in the house! Why didn't I have you guys come earlier?")

But you're not really "living" in "your home" anymore. Waiting for your buyer is a difficult way to exist -- with half a foot in your old house and half a foot out. The longer your house is on the market, the harder it becomes to sustain this way of life. I understand your discomfort and feel your pain … the only way to alleviate this feeling is to design the house to sell quickly and for top dollar.

Turn the page. Let's begin to stage.

Chapter Seven

The Devil Is in the Details

We're almost ready to begin staging your house for that all-important photo shoot and the first round of agents and buyers to walk through the front door. One more thing before you can put the pieces in position: Your home must go through a deep, deep, deep cleaning in order for the property to look like a model home and smell fresh. No real odor. No clutter. No dust bunnies. No footprint from you, the soon-to-be former owner. Our goal is neutral, open spaces that are *insanely* clean. This is the time to have the windows cleaned and screens stored to allow maximum light to shine throughout the house.

I realize that no one actually "lives" this clean, but you must try to exist in deep clean mode in order to sell. It begins with the first big clean, which is at a detailed level including removing the smudges and handprints on switch plates, stairway walls and doors. You will remove scuff marks on stairway treads and (finally) get that stain off the sink. Buyers don't want to see the evidence of your life or spot the crumbs in the corners of your drawers. Ick!

There is a psychology behind clean houses that helps in the home selling process. A study at Indiana University found that people perceived clean houses were linked to healthier individuals that lived in them while the flipside is, they associated messier homes with increased risk of disease. In fact, home cleanliness was even thought to be more of a predictor of physical health in humans than neighborhood features such as walking paths or gyms.

Three words: Clean it up. Dirt and mess will make potential buyers walk. No, make that *run*.

> **SMART MOVE:** Hire a cleaning service to do a detailed, thorough cleaning of the house. Schedule the window cleaning and store the screens.

Set The Interior Template

When staging a house - or what I call *setting the template* - you do not have to break the bank. This section will serve as the master guide to some of the most common inexpensive, cosmetic updates and home improvements that are done to increase the visual value of the house. I'll proceed logically room-by-room and also share with you my best staging secrets, tips and proven ways to design your house to sell.

On hand is all the furniture and accessories you are keeping or kept for staging purposes only. As we go through each room, you might find yourself moving a chair that was in one room to another because the proportion and/or color is better. It's important to keep an open mind during this process and look at how your furniture can be used in ways you've never considered. It will be an organic process for you, plus it's fun! (You might, however, be moving certain furniture or accessories to a storage area if they just don't fit.)

Before we start, let's take a moment to realize how far we've come. We compiled a list of issues that will be addressed both inside and out before you list your house to sell. We have agreed with your agent on a launch schedule that works and have chosen the date the house will be photographed, D-Day. The sorting, purging and packing process is complete. The storage decisions have been made. You are ready for the next critical step: Set the Template.

The Bare Bones

PAINT

Let's focus on the interior paint and assume that you have agreed to paint all walls throughout the house. I use only Benjamin Moore paints for the consistent quality and results.

PAINT DETAILS:
Wall Color:
- Navaho White (creamy, warm white)
- Classic Gray (cool, but warm gray)
- Finish: Eggshell

Trim:
- White Dove (for older homes)
- Simply White (for newer homes)
- Finish: Semi-Gloss or Satin

Ceilings:
- Ceiling White
- Finish: Flat

FLOORING

You've weighed the cost and benefit of replacing flooring, tile, carpet and area rugs. In older homes where wall-to-wall carpeting is covering hardwood floors, remove the carpeting, add shoe molding and polish up the floors. Done.

The Sisal/Berber blend carpeting from carpet stores or Home Depot is my favorite for great rooms and basements. It comes in several soft taupe colors and can also be used in the lighter cream color in bedrooms. It looks and feels like wool, but is actually Scotch-Guarded nylon and has a low, pile nub. Home Depot also offers a wide selection of area rugs to provide an inexpensive option for rooms that may need a rug. Get the look for less-much less.

Replace flooring with an inexpensive new laminate, luxury vinyl or engineered wood. Looks like classic hardwood without the maintenance and expense. It's resistant to scratches, stains and dents. Install it on top of the existing flooring, if possible, to save time and money.

Garage Floors

Many sellers will paint their garage floors gray. It does look finished and is a definite plus when selling a house. A gentle reminder that you will not be able to park a car on the painted surface for about 21 days while it dries. If you drive into the garage before it is truly dry, the paint will come off on your tire treads. Are you willing to park your car(s) outside the garage for 21 days?

FLOORING DETAILS:

- Replace or retile to showcase value in your flooring.
- Buff hardwood or use a floor product to restore the luster of the original finish.

LIGHTING

Check each lamp and fixture you own -- both inside and out -- to be sure that you are using soft white light bulbs of the correct style and wattage. My personal favorite is GE soft white light bulbs in 60 watts (minimum),100 or 50-100-150 watts depending on the lamp. Buyers want to see the spaciousness of the room with one quick glance. Poor lighting is noticeable and creates a negative impression on buyers. Purchase extra bulbs to have on hand when one blows out.

LIGHTING DETAILS:

- Remove window treatments and leave sheer curtains or plain windows.
- Replace non-white metal or non-working blinds.
- Hire a professional window cleaner.

THE PERFECT LISTING ™

FOYER

The foyer is a critical space in any style home; traditional, contemporary or transitional. If there is no real "foyer," but a small entrance to the house with no room for furniture, select a piece of artwork in the size and style that compliments the entrance. Showcase even a tiny space to make it look welcoming.

FOYER DETAILS:

- Place a chest or sofa table with a mirror above, lamp,

tray for keys, a candle and a white orchid.

- Move the family "drop zone." Identify new area(s) to store the everyday items you and your family will need to function while the house is on the market. Remove everyday items such as keys, papers, backpacks, mail and shoes.

LIVING ROOM

This is "the money shot" for many buyers and needs to be perfect. Make sure that there is a natural walking path through the room of at least two to two and a half feet of clear space. We do not want the buyer to feel physically or psychologically crowded or forced to look at the floor to avoid bumping into furniture, statues or small tables. We want their eyes focused on the room as a whole and notice the crown molding, recessed lighting, natural light and the possibilities that the room presents.

LIVING ROOM DETAILS:

- Identify the focal point in the room. When I bought my house, I knew that the focal point was the fireplace in the living room despite the fact that it was covered with this old and very kitschy Delft blue and white tile. There was a bank of three beautiful windows on the largest wall that looked out to the front yard and street. However, there was no large wall to place the sofa to create the main seating area.
- What to do? The first step was to add black 12 x 12 marble tile on top of the existing tile and place shoe

molding around the base of the fireplace to account for the raised tile. The second step was to install plantation shutters from Home Depot on the lower half of the three windows to create a visual wall and privacy from the street, so that you would not see the back of the sofa. Problem solved.

- Decide on your focal point if you do not have a fireplace. Create the focal point against the largest wall and balance the furniture in front of it. A well-chosen piece of artwork will complete the scene.

- Scale and proportion are key here. Remove any furniture or items that are too large or too small for the room's scale. Example: That overstuffed chair really looks better in the Great Room, which is a larger room.

- Create a simple furniture layout for the room starting with the largest pieces you have to work with: sofa or loveseat. Add chairs, coffee table, cubes or poof and side tables.

- I realize that many people have no prior experience with spatial relationships. That's why in our super-sized society, I'll frequently see a sofa that takes up more than half a room because it was purchased in a furniture store with 20-foot ceilings, or the sofa itself is over-sized. If a piece overwhelms the room, remove it.

- Sofa too big? Put it in storage and buy a $299 couch from Bob's Discount Furniture (or the equivalent in your area). Make sure it's a neutral color (taupe) with woven fabric in an updated style. Sofa the wrong color? Purchase a Sure Fit slipcover in taupe, cream or white.

- Remove area rugs that are too small for the room and replace with a larger rug or leave the hardwood floors bare. Hardwood floors equate to value in the mind of the buyer. I always say: "They're buying the floor and not the rug."

Should I Keep that Window Treatment?

Many living rooms have window treatments that are so heavy and luxurious (and often old) that you can never tell if the day has morphed into night. Elaborate, patterned or old-style draperies are seller specific, block natural light and darken an otherwise light room. Remove them.

- Let's go back to lighting. My basic rule is that in a typical living room, there are at least three to four 100-watt lamps in addition to overhead lighting. Lighting is an easy and inexpensive fix. Head to HomeGoods, TJ Maxx, Marshalls or Target to buy additional matching lamps to properly light the room.

- When it comes to color in pillows or throws or accessories remember my 60-30-10 rule. Your predominant color should occupy 60 percent of the visual, your accent color 30 percent and your punch color 10 percent.

- Intentionally add accessories to the coffee and side tables. I typically use coffee table books on art, architecture, travel, photography and design. The local Home Depot and grocery stores all carry $20 orchid plants in tasteful pots that fit nicely on tables. White orchids are the safest choice.

- Built-in bookcases are valuable to buyers, but very few people know how to design them to sell. I don't use soft-cover books, but gather hardcovers from other rooms in the house, a used book store or a local dollar store to stage. You do not need it to be full. No one can argue with well-organized books that are grouped together this way: three to five stand up straight while two lay down next to them with a little paperweight or accessory on top.

SMART MOVE: Purchase and place the correct style and size plant material to provide a tasteful accent near the entry, on tables, mantles and other surfaces that will serve as a focal point in the room.

DINING ROOM

Remember that if you're using this room for something else, you will need to convert it back into a functional dining room.

DINING ROOM DETAILS:

- Show the dining room table in a size proportionate to the dimensions of the room. Dining chairs will surround the table and a china cabinet or sideboard with a mirror will balance the visual heft of the table and chairs.
- Remove the leaf from the dining room table to create a smaller piece of furniture and thus make the room look more spacious.
- Limit the dining chairs (4-10) to fit logically with the

table size. Push the chairs in, so no one is bumping into them. If the room is large enough to accommodate, consider placing two side chairs on either side of the sideboard for visual balance.

- Recover dining room chair fabric that is stained and worn with neutral fabric in a soft geometric pattern or classic stripe.

- No table? Purchase an unfinished, wood composite table, neutral tablecloth and glass top from many online retailers like Ballard Designs. The 48-inch table, cloth and glass top are sold as a set for just under $300.

- Clean and polish the table. You can set it with your best silver and crystal or leave it unadorned. I like to place a crystal footed bowl on the table with an arrangement of white orchids, live moss and trailing ivy as an accent. This centerpiece is clean, beautiful and has a classic, lasting appeal.

- No chandelier? Home Depot offers a variety of inexpensive options for every style home. The chandelier does not need to *be* expensive, but must *look* as if it belongs in a house at this price point. I've hung $150 chandeliers in five million-dollar homes. No one would assume that it's glass or lower-quality crystal. They would assume that it's Waterford. And they did.

- China cabinets should feature one set of plates or crystal glassware to limit a visual that is distracting to buyers.

GREAT ROOM/FAMILY ROOM

As with the living room, the first step is to determine the focal point such as another fireplace, French doors or sliding glass door to the outdoors.

GREAT ROOM/FAMILY ROOM DETAILS:

- Place the furniture in a visually and physically logical format that highlights the width, depth and unique assets of the room. You will use the sofa, side chairs, tables, lamps, coffee table and large area rug to create the main seating area.
- This room will be set up much like the living room's main seating area. Remove extra furniture that is not critical or blocks the natural path to and from the room.
- Built-in shelves and cabinets should feature hardcover books and few generic accents in keeping with the color scheme and style of the room. The shelves do not have to be full, but rather accented with books to show the value of the built-ins and the availability of storage and display.
- Televisions on top of cabinets or built-ins can stay as a focal point across from the seating area.
- Remove or hide the visual chaos of TV, cable and gaming cords from view.
- Visually contain all clutter collections such as DVDs, CDs, toys, games, magazines and extra books.

KITCHEN

They say that the kitchen is the "heart of the home." *They* are right, which means that this room is critical to the ultimate sale of the home. It must look and feel clean, functional and bright. To upgrade the look and feel of your own kitchen, examine the following areas to visually and physically upgrade.

KITCHEN DETAILS:

- Severely limit what you keep on the countertops to include essentials like the coffee maker, knife block and matching flour, sugar and tea canisters. Pack or remove the rest.
- Appliances should all be in perfect working order. Kitchens should highlight the appliances – fridge, stove, dishwasher, microwave, oven – and they should visually match. Nothing looks worse than that black fridge with white stove and beige dishwasher. If the color of the appliances doesn't match, but all are in working order, consider ordering a new front panel to match the color of the other appliances. I once ordered a stainless panel cut at a sheet metal company to install on a white Sub-Zero refrigerator for $700. Savings = thousands. **SMART MOVE.**
- It is critical that the appliance brands match the price point of the house. You don't have to put a new Sub-Zero fridge in a lower priced home, but it might be necessary in a more expensive one.

- Countertops: I rarely replace them. If possible, work with what you have in place. Steam clean the grout on a tiled countertop or replace with pre-cut melamine countertops sold at The Home Depot in a neutral.

- Marble, Granite or Silestone? Polish to remove surface stains.

- Butcher block has burned rings into the wood? Sand and refinish.

- Consider a countertop replacement versus a bigger and more expensive paint job. Example: A recent seller had an older kitchen with dark cabinets, dark hardware and dark granite countertops. They told me that they planned to paint the cabinets. The cost of painting these top of the line wood cabinets in this particular kitchen was many thousands of dollars. I stood back and realized that the cabinet color was not as distracting and dated as the dark granite color, which drew your eye immediately. In the end, we replaced the granite in a soft taupe color that updated the overall look of the kitchen and the eye naturally looked right past the dark kitchen cabinets to the beautiful French doors that opened onto the back patio.

- Repaint cabinet doors white with Benjamin Moore's White Dove or Simply White. Even if the cabinets are old in size and style, white doors will visually enlarge the space. You do not have to paint the interior of the cabinets, but remove old shelf liner and scrub clean.

- When replacing drawer and door hardware select the size and style that will provide an updated look and feel.
- Consider installing under-cabinet lights for an additional light source.
- Steam clean or replace grout and caulk.
- Make sure all cabinets, drawers and pantry are clean and organized.
- Remove old curtains or blinds.
- You can leave an organized command center where the phone is located.
- Add a bowl of fresh fruit on the counter as an accent. I only use Granny Smith (green apples) because they're inexpensive, always look fresh and add a pop of color. Thirteen apples creates a nice pile in a bowl-remember to remove the numbered grocery sticker on each apple.

What STILL Might Need to Go from Your Kitchen

- All calendars
- School and club directories
- Family photos
- Art projects
- Basket of letters and bills
- 1000 cookbooks
- Old dish towels
- Worn wooden spoons and other cooking utensils that sit out
- Worn oven mitts and hot pads
- Medicine and vitamins
- Magnets and papers attached to the fridge
- Nine thousand plastic food flippers and spatulas
- Nine million appliances you never use
- Broken small appliances that you plan to fix "someday"

Clean Naturally

As you continue to live in the house during the sales process move toward more natural ways of keeping it clean. A great way to clean your kitchen and bathroom is mixing seven cups of water with ½ cup of baking soda and 1/3 a cup of lemon juice, plus ¼ cup of vinegar in a bowl or bucket. Soak your sponges in this mixture for cleaning. It's also an amazing grout cleaner when used with an old toothbrush.

• Consider hiring a professional cleaning crew for a deep kitchen clean and focus on making the stovetop, oven and inside of the fridge look brand new.

MASTER BEDROOM

Buyers are looking for a sanctuary and are willing to pay for perfection in the master bedroom.

MASTER BEDROOM DETAILS:

• Furniture should include a queen or king-sized bed, two nightstands with lamps, a dress and a mirror - space allowing.

• A proportionate sized piece of artwork over the bed presents a finished look.

• The bed will be your biggest piece of furniture. Make sure it's placed on the largest continuous wall to allow for a well-balanced room.

• Invest in a clean white or cream matelassé coverlet and matching shams. Avoid using too many patterns and mismatched colors as they will distract the buyer and not photograph well. No bed skirt? Buy one in a white or cream box pleat style at Target for less than $20.

• If there is room, a tasteful seating area is a wonderful

selling point. It can feature one or two chairs or a loveseat and small table.

- A few accent pillows on the bed or loveseat in a style and color in keeping with the overall design of the room is a great investment. Head to HomeGoods, TJ Maxx, Marshalls or Target for hundreds of choices in size, style and color.

- A mirror over the dresser will make the room appear larger.

- Use at least three to four, 100-watt lamps in the room. Place one on each bedside table and one or two on the dresser. Not enough lamps? Check the rest of the lamps in the house to see if the style and color can be used in the master.

- Master closet should look like it was done by a pro. What's left isn't much, but it's clean and beautifully folded and hung with order facing in the same direction. Buyers resonate with organization, order and perfection.

- Remove personal clutter on all surfaces- knick-knacks, tissue boxes, pills, magazines and water bottles. Leave clocks and remotes.

- Don't block windows with furniture or heavy window covering draperies. Allow in the natural light.

> **SMART MOVE**: Remove off season clothes, shoes and accessories to showcase room in a closet. When the space appears half full, it gives the impression that there is so much space that you don't use it all and they won't either.

OTHER BEDROOMS

Each bedroom should mimic the master.

BEDROOM DETAILS:
- Bedrooms should contain the same basic furniture including a side table or nightstand, lamps, chest or dresser, mirror, artwork and area rug.
- The bed is typically the largest piece of furniture in the room, so make sure that it's on the correct wall. If you're unsure, it may be the largest wall with at least one outlet.
- If you have a small room consider a daybed against the wall.
- No bed? No problem. Intex air mattresses are available in all bed sizes at Target. When placed on top of six small moving boxes, this will work if you cover them in a white or ivory bed skirt, matelassé coverlet and bed pillows with matching shams. Don't forget to purchase the pump!
- Have the right number of lamps with the correct type and wattage light bulbs and open the curtains or blinds as much as possible to let in natural light.
- Remove broken ceiling fans and replace with a flush

mount fixture with a brushed nickel rim. My favorite from Home Depot is sold with one, 60-watt bulb or two 60-watt bulbs. Plenty of light.

- Toy storage chests are inexpensive and will contain all the bedroom toys. Put the toys away when a buyer is on the way.
- Bookcases should contain books, plus a few decorative items, if any.

BATHROOMS

All bathrooms need to be squeaky clean, well-lit and updated when possible if it fits your budget. The Home Depot is a one-stop bathroom mecca of style, finish and price for the following updates. If you choose not to update, there are tips below for you, too:

BATHROOM DETAILS:
UPDATES:

- If necessary, install new vanities and countertop combos in white. Home Decorators Collection has great basics.
- If needed, install new faucets. Kohler 4-inch or 8-inch spreads are my go-to picks.
- If you must remodel, new toilets and sinks in white from Kohler are my top choices.
- Use 4 x 4 or 12 x 12 white ceramic wall tile with coordinating accent pieces if your tile is old or broken.
- Floor tile in 12 x 12 ceramic or marble are a perfect choice.

- Install mirrored medicine cabinets that are surface mounted. Replace older, smaller medicine cabinets with the updated version that features a mirror with a beveled edge.
- Light fixtures come in two, three or four light selections. Install for an updated look with higher light capacity.
- Install new hardware. Towel bars in 18 inches and 24 inches, towel ring, toilet paper holder and robe hooks are all sold in sets in different styles and finishes by Delta, Kohler, Moen and Glacier Bay, among other brands.
- Replace cloudy shower doors if they are cracked or cannot be cleaned.
- Remove old shower sliding doors and replace with a new shower curtain rod.

SMALLER FIXES:

- Replace all caulking around tubs, shower and sink if cracked or moldy.
- Purchase and install new shower curtain liner in clear or white; curtain should be in white matelassé or waffle weave and new curtain rings in brushed nickel.
- Purchase new white towels to display. This is critical to complete the updated look you are creating. You will use the old towels by folding them neatly and storing under the cabinet during showings. The master will need two white bath towels and two white hand towels; other bathrooms need one of each.

- Purchase a new white bathroom rug. You will not show it on D-Day, but during showings as it will coordinate with and complete the bathroom.
- Place a crystal or ceramic dish with a guest soap on the sink of each bathroom.
- Vanity counter space in the master bath? Consider a silver tray with crystal perfume bottles, a crystal jewelry dish and a small candle.
- Add artwork over the back of the toilet or on the wall to complete the perfect visual.
- Store all personal items below the sink or in a small plastic caddy that can travel with you from the bedroom to the bathroom each day.
- Clean shower and tub daily with one-part water and one-part bleach. Don't forget to spray down tile walls to avoid mold and mildew.
- Reminder: Don't use the guest soap and display towels!

LAUNDRY ROOM

For this multi-purpose and utilitarian room, think bright, clean and neutral. Room for a wrapping station or gift gallery? It does not take much to create the possibility that today's buyer will identify with. Showcase the space and possibility.

LAUNDRY ROOM DETAILS:

- Washing machine and dryer must be functional, properly vented and have adequate drainage into a laundry sink.

- Reglaze a cast iron sink or purchase a new hard plastic laundry sink or sink/cabinet combo from Home Depot.
- Replace faucet if necessary.
- Replace bare, hanging bulbs with a thin fluorescent fixture to provide more light.
- Paint the floor a taupe or gray to match the carpeting next door in the lower level family room if the laundry is a separate room.
- New countertops? White melamine that are pre-cut from Home Depot will do the trick.
- Paint old cabinets in Benjamin Moore White Dove or remove them entirely.
- Update door knobs and drawer handles with brushed nickel or chrome. Be sure to measure the width of the actual holes for drawer pulls before replacing as older cabinets used smaller pulls.
- Consider painting the floor a taupe or gray or retile it for a fresh look. If you have older tile in there, you can tile the new right over the old to reduce cost.
- Purchase metal shelving units to accommodate laundry soaps, cleaning supplies, tools, lightbulbs, bulk pantry items and other items you would store in this room.
- Sort and pack all non-laundry essentials.

BASEMENT AND BONUS SPACE

No one even refers to them as basements or finished attics and nook-like rooms anymore. They're "lower level family rooms" and "the third floor". Sounds better, right? These are considered "bonus" spaces, and if clean, bright with polished floors or newly carpeted, they will give the house an edge when compared with similar listings in price point, size, style and location. These bonus spaces do not need to be staged and can be left vacant if the main floor, bedrooms and bathrooms are visually and physically perfect. If the rest of the house is not perfectly presented, you will define the spaces (office, guest bedroom, playroom, etc.) and finish them using the guidelines we have created for other rooms.

BASEMENT AND BONUS SPACE DETAILS:
- Paint
- Lighting
- Carpet
- Done

GARAGE

The rule of thumb for garages is the same for any other usable area inside of your home. You must be able to see the width and depth of the room and immediately understand its primary use and storage capability. The lighting must be adequate, and the garage door and door openers must be functional.

GARAGE DETAILS:

- Power wash all walls and floors.
- Repair any foundation cracks.
- If necessary, repaint walls with waterproof or water sealant paint.
- Paint garage floor gray if parking outside for 21 days is possible. (See sidebar on Page 101)
- Use shelving to organize all critical garage items you will need to keep.
- Update lighting fixture if needed.
- Pack up car supplies, mouse traps, bug spray, old projects, toys and store.

Set the Exterior Template

Remember that buyers are going through their mental checklist the moment they pull up in front of your home. It follows that all outdoor areas must be pristine, inviting and welcoming. Let's work on kicking up your curb appeal.

The Bare Bones

EXTERIOR DETAILS:

- Exterior: Paint house and trim if paint is peeling or faded.
- Roof: Power wash to remove algae build up. Replace missing shingles.
- Chimney: Replace cracked and missing brick, stone or mortar.

- Shutters: Sand and paint existing or replace with vinyl sets.
- Railings: Sand and spray paint wrought iron railings with a wire brush and a can of Rustoleum black spray paint from Home Depot.

LIGHTING:

- Replace exterior lighting that is inadequate or dated. Clean fixtures and use the correct type and wattage bulbs.
- Purchase inexpensive, battery operated lights for under $20 each to place in front of bushes or along paths. Replace or remove old, non-working path lights.

LANDSCAPING:

- Trim all trees and landscaping that block the front façade of the house.
- Need a quick new front garden bed? Use eight or nine-foot Holly trees to frame the outer edges of the house. Plant a row of four-foot Cherry Laurel bushes in the front along the left and right sides of the door. Create a focal point. Add three Boxwood trees in a triangle pattern on either side of the path to the front door and finish with green or Variegated Liriope.
- Remove dead trees, limbs, shrubs and plant material. Edge all gardens and spread with brown mulch-not red or black.
- Place one to two proportionately sized urns on the

front stoop. Stick with seasonal flowers including large white pansies in spring and fall or small Boxwood shrubs during the dead of winter. Geraniums with green ivy is a clean look with a pop of a vibrant red or pink color during summer months. A small Boxwood, large white pansies and green ivy is my "go-to" combination for outdoor front and back planters.

- Use the rule of 3:1 for pots. The large or tall plant as the center plant, medium size plant to surround the center and a trailing vine as the accent plant.

- No privacy from the neighbors? Purchase and install a row of 7-8 feet American Holly trees or Cherry Laurel shrubs. This is lower in cost than installing a permanent fence and creates a tasteful privacy screen.

- Keep the lawn mowed, watered and free of leaves and storm debris. Lawn should have clean, clear edges. Fill in yellowed or bare spots with sod or seed.

- If drainage beds under decks or in the yard are filled with small stones add to volume so that it looks full.

- Store garden hoses and sprinklers in the garage.

FRONT DOOR:

- Replace house numbers with Baldwin four-inch polished brass, nickel or black. Nowhere to put them? Purchase an unpainted oval wooden plaque and paint it the color of front door and shutters. Attach the Baldwin brass, nickel or black numbers on the front of the plaque and screw placque directly into the brick or siding. You will now see the house numbers clearly from the street.

- Repaint or restain the front door and update the hardware to reflect visual security and the price point of the house. For the well-dressed door, you will need: knocker, mail slot, handset and kick plate. Home Depot sells various styles and finishes from both Schlage and Kwikset. Door color can be a classic black or red.

- Purchase new, outdoor coir-style mats for each exterior door in a plain or classic bordered style.

CLEANING:

- Power wash exterior brick or siding to remove green algae and moss.

- Power wash all decks, patios, and pool decks. For wooden decks, sand and restain if necessary.

- Power wash all exterior structures and patio furniture.

OUTDOOR FURNITURE:

- Create conversation areas with furniture and tables. No outdoor furniture? Borrow from a friend or neighbor.

FINAL TOUCHES:

- Limit the outdoor eye candy: Bird feeders, bird baths, statues, sculpture, fountains, urns and large toys. Place a single birdbath, statue or set of urns with meaningful intention to create focal points or areas you want to highlight in the backyard.

- Remove the pet poop daily.
- Touch up outdoor furniture with paint or spray paint.
- Replace a broken or faded umbrella.
- Remove sandbags that you're using to redirect water.
- Swap out moldy, old-looking cushions. Purchase new accent pillows for a pop of color from Home Depot, HomeGoods, TJ Maxx, Marshalls or Target.
- Move your grill to the side of the house if visual and physical space is limited. Clean your outdoor kitchen grill. Store cooking tools.

Congratulations! You did it! Your home is ready for that first group of buyers.

But wait... what's next?

Chapter Eight

The Sound of Time

The goal was to design the house to appeal to the potential buyer. You've done that. The emotional roller coaster is back at the station, and you are ready to unbuckle your safety harness and jump off the ride. You are physically and emotionally exhausted and your credit cards are out of commission. That said, you are relieved that the most labor-intensive part of the process is finally over. The overall impression you have created is a positive one that highlights the unique assets of your house while focusing the eye away from its liabilities.

The house is 100 percent clean and the rooms are well-designed and without clutter. The challenge now is to actually "live" day-to-day while maintaining the perfection you have created. We've discussed that this artificial environment is incompatible with how you actually live and will be truly challenging to maintain over time. But, think of it this way: The perfection you will maintain is for good reason, which is to sell the house quickly and for top dollar. It will be worth it.

D-Day is here...finally. It's time for the great reveal and you are ready to showcase your back breaking work and updated asset to your Realtor.

The Normal Sequence of Events

At this point it's common for the agent to schedule your house on the office's weekly tour of new listings. After this "first tour," the agent may ask their colleagues to suggest a list price or price range based on this tour. The agent will share this information with you in spite of the fact that **you** will actually decide on the list price, not them. In addition, your agent might host a morning coffee, buffet lunch or cocktail preview where the office agents can bring qualified buyers to view the listing before it hits the MLS. Other agents use the Friday before the weekend open house to schedule showings by appointment only.

Many homes do sell this way, which is why it is done and thus reduces the days on the market to zero. If you prepared your asset to sell and you're lucky, this means no disruptive showings! It obviously does not happen with regularity for most listings, which is why you will most likely proceed to Plan B.

You wait.

No one can predict how long the sales process will take. It's based on the location, presentation and the price point of your house, the current market, the time of year, and the number of qualified buyers that show serious interest. Your job is to WAIT for your agent to present an offer for you to consider and make a decision. Until then, keep calm, maintain the perfection of the house each day and let your agent do his or her job.

In the next few days, your house will be entered into the MLS and officially on the market. Your agent is thrilled with the work that you have done and excited to present the new listing to the public. Their job is to expertly market your house and find that buyer. **How will you cope with living in a house that's on the market? It will get harder the longer you do it. That's why I ask: Can you hear it? It's the sound of time.**

Ticking. Ticking. Ticking.

Yoga breaths! Slowly inhale and just as slowly...exhale. (But don't self-soothe with a shopping trip to the mall. The last thing you need is more stuff to pack!)

Yes, it's an artificial and stressful way to live, but you will get through it. Everyone does. Remember the old adage: "This too shall pass." True, this is an inconvenience, but also a means to an end. The "end" is a ratified contract, home inspection and a closing date.

It's helpful during this stressful waiting period to give yourself fun activities and distractions in order to break up the time. A visit to Mom and Dad in another state or sending the kids to grandma's for two weeks of summer break is just the ticket. Even a staycation at a local hotel will be a welcome mental and physical break during a time when you're feeling overtired, overworked and totally displaced. Go to the gym. Really. It's a great way to lower your blood pressure.

Acknowledge the stress and allow yourself to move through it. It's normal and expected. You have removed all the emotional and physical ivy that made your house a home. Think about it: You don't currently have a real home base anymore, which is unsettling. Susan Clayton, an environmental psychologist at the College of Wooster, found that for many human beings their home is part of their self-definition and what they place in their home is an extension of themselves. You're emotionally between homes during this transition, which might make you feel a little panicky. It's common.

Realize that during this time, the routine you established and relied upon each day will be non-existent. You won't be functioning at your highest capacity and your family will be all twisted up. Even the dog is acting weird. (Here's some interesting news: It actually takes a year to really settle in physically and emotionally and to feel like yourself after a move).

But back to the wait. I have a client whose property sat on the market for 13 months. Each and every day as she lived there and waited, she had to clean up after herself until the house was perfect again. At the same time, she was painting her new co-op in New York City and dealing with a difficult co-op board. Was she freaking out? Not exactly. She wished her property would sell and did everything possible to make that happen but accepted that the roller coaster ride would continue until her current house sold. What helped her keep it together and stay positive was knowing that *the wait* was just another part of the process.

Living in limbo without our normal creature comforts is an incredibly difficult situation for most people, so you need to treat yourself with some TLC while making sure that the Perfect Listing™ stays just that...perfect.

And then the phone rings.

The Emotional Roller Coaster Rolls On

This can be a time of incredible highs, especially when your agent says the magic words, "I have an offer." It can also be a time of incredible

CAROLINE CARTER | 129

lows when a buyer's agent tries to convince you and your agent why they're presenting an extremely solid, but lowball offer. Your job as the seller is to wait, and wait and wait to say one of two little words: yes or no.

You're in a virtual no man's land of uncertainty as you wonder what each day will bring. You have to keep your emotions in check as your Realtor shares negative feedback from agents and buyers about your house. You might hear that the kitchen "is small and dumpy" while the upstairs "looks cramped." Remember, it's all individual perspective as the next buyer calls it "charming, cozy, and just what I wanted." You can't take any of it personally. TRULY. Remain calm. Inhale. Exhale.

SOLD!

There will come the day when you get the call from your agent that you have been expecting since listing your house for sale. The offer is amazing; the buyer has cash and the closing date is doable. You discuss it for a few moments, but you know that the answer is one word: YES! Your hard work has paid off because your house now has a ratified contract and will soon go through a home inspection! Congratulations! This is a truly joyous moment in life. It's also a sobering one.

This is actually happening. You no longer live here. You are moving on.

Now, it's time to enter the next phase of the transition process and schedule your move. Do you hear the metal on metal of the roller coaster ramping up again as you inch up those high tracks only to start screaming on your way down?

Chapter Nine

The Red Zone

Welcome to the Red Zone. It's a gridiron football term used when the football is within twenty yards of the goal – almost there -- but even such lofty placement doesn't guarantee success. The team still has to continue with our strategic guide to ensure the rest of the transition proceeds according to plan. We've come this far, and we want the TD!

Speaking of red …

You have a closing date and it's circled in red on your calendar. It's time to finally find a moving company and transition your household goods. This choice is critical and the key to the success or failure of your overall move experience. Will your move go smoothly or be one of those disaster stories that you talk about for the next ten years to anyone who will listen?

In other words: Do your homework and choose a moving company wisely so you won't have the same experience as a friend who watched her movers get into a physical fight on her old front lawn and had to dial 911 when one stabbed the other with his pen. Moving! The gift that keeps on giving.

The Moving Industry

It is very confusing to compare and select a mover. It has always been that way – and there is no change in the foreseeable future.

Uneducated sellers shop estimates and many decide to hire movers based on price alone. It's very difficult to understand individual moving companies' pricing strategies, estimates, insurance options, and surcharges. Many companies still compile hand-written estimates and hand-written numbered inventories that take a genius to decipher. Technology has not been fully integrated across the industry, so it does not always serve home sellers in a transparent and helpful way.

Good news flash: This will change in time, but the industry -- a good ol' boys network that needs more women--is not there yet. So, you need to understand how to compare "apples to apples." Your moving options are many and include national and international carriers, Three Guys and a Truck and your son and his friends who just started their own company.

Where do you start and how do you decide which company to hire?

Apples to Apples

Comparing apples to apples and oranges to oranges here is crucial. This means you have the estimator provide you with a complete financial picture including all service options, potential upcharges, and surprises you may encounter during your move.

Sure, that mover costs $1,000 for a basic move, but there are additional charges that make the price soar thousands of dollars based on weight, location, and moving difficult or specialty items. Lay out your entire move and ask for the bottom line cost. Then go back, read the fine print, read it again, and ask if XYZ is included. It's typical to hear, "Oh, I forgot to advise you about ..."

Rely on word-of-mouth. Each city and town has two or three great moving companies. Families engage them repeatedly with consistent success. There are two in the Washington, D.C. area that I've used consistently over the years. I know their crews, their pricing structure and that their promise of excellent service is delivered, and client concerns and insurance claims are handled immediately. It makes the move so much easier if you have someone who knows the level of perfection you expect and recommends a moving company that will meet your expectations.

Now, let's go back to the cost for a moment.

As with most things in life: You get what you pay for. A lot of sellers think they're just moving their things from Point A to Point B and want to save money. They don't consider all the aspects of the move, and why it's often better to pay a bit more for a more comprehensive or alternative service.

Start with the fact that movers will give you an estimate based on counting your pieces of furniture to calculate the cubic square footage of the items, which is then converted into weight and multiplied by price. It's important to note that there is no standardized pricing for a home move or how each mover calculates their estimate. There are, however, common factors to consider. The veteran movers will carry a clipboard with an estimate sheet, pen, and calculator; newer movers will use a fancy, handheld device to do their estimate. The devices still basically count the individual pieces of furniture, convert to cubic feet and weight to estimate basic cost and labor needed to complete the move.

There are industry standards for tariffs when it comes to moving, but hourly rates are all over the place. Another interesting fact to keep in mind is that the moving companies don't always make their profit on the actual moves. They make considerable income and profit on packing supplies and storage. Buyer beware!

The actual cost of labor has become so competitive that in order to survive in this industry, many moving companies continue to raise their hourly pay rates to retain movers who aren't even loyal to their company. Newer companies may offer to pay a higher hourly rate to attract talent, but that doesn't ensure that their workers are any more professional or experienced. Check the status and length of service of the company's existing labor force and what percentage of workers are employees versus contract workers. Clarify this by asking the company representative who is providing your estimate.

Insurance

It's helpful to review insurance options in detail as the number one question movers are asked is: What are you liable for during the move?

The answer is your mover is liable for the value of the goods you have hired them to transport from Point A to Point B, *but* there are varying levels of liability to consider. You will choose the level of liability needed to determine the replacement cost if an item is lost or damaged. Federal law requires moving companies to offer two levels of liability insurance. They are described in greater detail below. If you run into a moving company that doesn't offer coverage -- show them the door.

Here are your choices:

Full Value Protection. You pay an additional fee, so that your mover is liable for the *replacement* value of lost and/or damaged goods in your entire shipment. This is the more comprehensive plan available for the protection of your belongings. If any item is lost, destroyed, or damaged while in your mover's custody then your mover will, at their discretion, offer to do one of the following for each item:

- Repair the item.
- Replace with a similar dollar value item.
- Make a cash settlement for the cost of the repair or the current market replacement value.

It's important to know that movers are permitted to limit their liability for loss or damage to articles of extraordinary value, unless you specifically list these articles on the transport document. An article of extraordinary value exceeds $100 per pound and might include jewelry, silverware, china, antiques, artwork and sculpture. It is important that you ask your mover for a written explanation of their limitations of liability before moving day. Ask your mover to give you, in writing, the details of their Full Value Protection Plan.

Released Value Protection. This plan is offered at no additional charge. It's a gamble because your protection is minimal. Your mover will assume liability for no more than 60 cents per pound per article. What does that mean to you? Let's say your mover drops your expensive stereo unit. It's 10 pounds when weighed and valued at $1,000. Now, it's in a million pieces on the sidewalk outside your new house. You will receive 60 cents times 10 pounds to replace it or $600, which might not be enough to buy a new unit. It's certainly not enough to replace the unit with the exact make and model that was damaged. Just remember, you're being paid according to the *weight* of the item and not the value. Ask for clarification in writing to review before choosing this option.

Third-Party Insurance. Some movers will also offer (for a fee) a separate liability insurance policy that's not included in the basic move package. It's optional insurance and must be offered by state law. This means your mover is still only liable for 60 cents per pound, but the rest of the loss can be recovered from the third-party insurance company. You can also purchase your own insurance from a third-party.

> **SMART MOVE:** Check your homeowner's insurance policy to see what is covered during the packing and transport portion of the move before purchasing supplemental insurance. Nothing of great value? No problem. Irreplaceable? Protect it.

Beyond insurance, movers might offer a more competitive base price for the actual move, but they may recoup the lost income in other ways, which is why you need to read the fine print on moving contracts. Or, have someone like me read it on your behalf. You'll need to know that they add a surcharge if the truck is X amount of feet from the street or there are X number of stairs to the front door. They will not release your load unless you pay those extra charges, which should be understood up front, but often falls between the cracks.

Another huge profit source for moving companies is packing

supplies, which they buy in bulk from wholesalers and pass along to clients with a minimum of 50 to 100 percent upcharge. As I previously discussed, warehouse storage is 100 percent profit for them if they have the space. They are happy to place your household items into seven by seven foot, wooden, pre-made crates, placed on large shelves in their warehouse and begin racking up big dollars, month after month, as people often leave the crates for a longer period of time, even years. Out of sight. Out of mind.

Once again, how do you pick the right mover? I typically start with referrals and reputation. Movers are not all created equally, so ask around. A good mover is customer-focused and detail-oriented in practice. They will lay folded boxes underneath the truck ramp to protect your slate walk or grass and place neoprene moving runners throughout the house to protect your floors. They wrap the stair railings in your house and wear booties inside instead of shoes when possible. Seek out and demand this type of service. You don't want them to mark your new wood floors with salt on their shoes when it's snowing. A good mover will be respectful of both your old and new home and treat it with the utmost care.

No two moving companies will prepare their estimate in the same way. For example, a company may only move certain things in your home for that low base price and the rest is extra (or they might not do it at all). Understand how to compare estimates.

It's crucial that you review what services each mover is actually offering for that estimate. For example, do you know *exactly* what your mover will and will not move? Don't assume.

And Just Plain Big Things

Legally, movers don't have to take everything you own and will not take certain things including hazardous materials, playsets, trampolines and other large items that have to be disassembled only to be reassembled at the new house. Your $5,000 exercise machine is something your movers probably won't touch. And they shouldn't. Knowing this in advance will mean that you can hire an expert to take it apart, transport it and then put it together at the new house. This is especially true of Total Gyms, Peloton bikes and treadmills and other valuable gym equipment.

These specialty vendors will move the items that most movers don't want to deal with to avoid the potential damage and legal liability. Quite often, I'll hire an authorized dealer of a particular valuable exercise machine to move it. If you have a piano, a mover will probably move it although it's much safer to reach out to an actual piano mover that will properly pack, transport and store it. Plan ahead for bigger items like a large slate pool table or above ground hot tub – two things many movers may not take even if you beg or bribe them. Or maybe they will take them for an enormous surcharge. Find out.

Movers do not have to move your wine. If your wine cellar is filled with costly bottles, you may have already arranged with experts who know exactly how to pack and transport your wine to protect against breakage and temperature differentials. Be sure to call ahead of time to book this service. Packing a wine cellar correctly is an art best left to these services and specialty stores that specifically address this all-important (for wine lovers) room of your home.

SMART MOVE: Understand clearly which items you own that are subject to a surcharge in advance. Know the exact dollar amount and get the quote in writing.

There is usually such a surcharge to rent pre-fabricated crates or to build individualized crates to transport large art, sculptures and lighting fixtures. Many movers that serve clients in high income areas with warehouse space to store them do offer ready-made crates to transport lighting fixtures. This service is usually offered at a nominal charge to the client as the crates are reusable. But remember, a mover will not disconnect your lighting fixtures; you will need an electrician to do so. Artwork and sculpture may require crates to be built to specification. When deciding on whether to contact an expert to pack and transport specialty items, consider the replacement cost of the item. Often, there is no discussion necessary. I will always hire the specialist. While the cost of engagement adds to the overall cost of the move, if your chandelier is worth $40,000, you are more concerned about securely packing and safety in transport than you are with the cost to build a $300 crate. Peace of mind is priceless.

This is what I call comparing apples to apples and oranges to oranges. One mover might seem cheaper, but the move estimate is basic without the surcharges necessary for your move. Another mover might have a higher base charge, but the surcharges are included. Confusing.

Educate yourself, make decisions based on apples to apples services, customer satisfaction ratings and referrals from friends and experts -- not bottom-line cost only.

Read, Read, Read The Fine Print

As with any contract, I implore you to read the fine print. Watch out for the following:

- The moving company is not liable if you've packed perishable, dangerous or hazardous materials in your boxes without the movers' knowledge.

- They might try to get out of their overall liability if you have packed your own boxes, which is referred to as a CP (Consumer Pack) or PBO (Packed by Owner). Some movers put into their contracts that if you packed your goods then you're also on the line if they are damaged. Unbelievable? Well, it's certainly a way to sell their packing services. Ask to have this clause deleted from your contract.

- They might say they're not liable if you fail to notify your mover in writing about articles of extraordinary value.

- They might try to walk away from liability if you sign the delivery receipt for your goods which discharges your mover or its agents from liability. By law, you have nine months to file a written claim. Strike anything else from your contract. Refuse to sign the delivery paperwork unless you have a proper receipt giving you the nine months to file a claim.

Timing = Money

It costs more to move during the summer months. Why? It's when the large majority of moves are scheduled and moving companies can and do charge a premium during these months. I realize that most people may not have a choice with a move date, especially with a job relocation or diplomatic posting. However, there are fewer moves during the winter months, so the price dips. Ask and you shall receive a discount!

Most families want to move when schools let out in June to enjoy summer in the new digs before the littles trot off to the buses again. Another popular time for moving is during the holiday season, specifically the week between Christmas Day and New Year's Day. I think that timing is a bit crazy, but when you need to move… you move, and obviously not everyone celebrates the same holidays.

The first week of January is also a popular week to move before the family returns to school and work. After mid-January, the number of moves dramatically tapers off until early spring. The middle of the month may be easier to schedule than towards the end. One word of caution about winter moves where snow, ice, and sleet are a factor: Plan for potential weather delays. Rain will also slow travel and create headaches when even the most carefully padded furniture is being soaked. Plan for extra time. And extra patience.

Movers will remind you that *you're* the one who will pay for the delays. When you enter into a contract with your mover, you will agree upon a day when your household goods are to be picked up and delivered to your new home. You (the one who is moving) determines that date and the date you require delivery. The mover will confirm that delivery date, or range of dates with a long-distance move. You or your trusted representative must be available on that day.

If you are not present or it is not possible to deliver due to closing delays or construction delays with the new house, it will cost you. A moving company has little choice but to hold the shipment overnight on the truck or store it at your expense at their warehouse. If the mover is unable to make the pickup or delivery then they must tell you by phone, telegram or in person. Telegram? I did mention that the moving industry is slow to change. You will then need to come to an agreement on a new delivery date.

This can easily happen with a new build. You've rushed to hire the movers based on a certain expected and agreed upon completion date and things change. It's not a tragedy. But it will cost you.

Ask your movers to clearly explain where your things will be held if there is a delay between loading and unloading dates. Where is the truck parked? Is there a security guard? Locked gates? Alarmed doors?

Your entire life is on that truck.

Moving is expensive. The American Moving and Storage Association states that the average cost of an out of state household move is around $4,300 for a distance of 1,225 miles while an interstate move costs about $2,300 for four movers at $200 per hour, or $50 per hour each laborer.

Local movers charge on an hourly basis regardless of the task at hand -- packing, carrying your boxes outside, loading the boxes into a truck, driving to a new destination, unloading your things, carrying your furniture pieces and boxes or even unpacking your things, which I advise against, but more on that later. Ask to see details of the hourly rates for their service. Keep a copy in writing and put it in your transition binder.

SMART MOVE Moving Details:

- Check documents to be sure that your movers are properly licensed, bonded and insured.
- Ask for an on-site-binding written estimate. A verbal quote might sound fine, but you don't want a quote over the phone that turns out to be thousands more when the estimator actually comes to the house.
- Clarify surcharges and extra costs to disassemble and reassemble furniture pieces. Be clear about their policy regarding overtime, parking permits, parking tickets and long carry fees.
- Ask your mover if the company is a member of the American Moving and Storage Association, which keeps them abreast of the changes and best practices in their industry.
- Check that your cross-country movers have a U.S. Department of Transportation number issued by the Federal Motor Carrier Safety Administration.
- Review the tariffs. What does this mean to you? Your moving company must set up and maintain a tariff, a document that contains all of the moving company rates, charges and service terms for moving a customer's household possession. This tariff must be made available for a customer's review. Tariffs must be clear and easy to follow.
- Clarify the labor crew you expect. Do they have the manpower to handle your move? In the peak summer

months, many movers are short staffed, which means they may need to hire seasonal contract workers to complete the uptick in moves. These new workers may lack the experience and skills to be thorough, carefully trained, expert movers. Make it clear in writing that you want and expect a professional, well-trained and seasoned crew.

- Make sure they have a positive safety and client track record. Ask how long they've been in business. Longevity doesn't mean they're necessarily a good mover, although it would be hard to maintain a business long term that does not serve the customer. Be wary if their Yelp and Google reviews are negative. Check the BBB to see if they have any consumer complaints pending.

- Confirm that your move will not be subcontracted to a third-party mover. Make sure they are solely responsible for the move and won't give your assignment away to other companies, which should be a red flag and potential contract breaker. Get this in writing.

- Make sure your moving company is insured against injuries. Take this seriously because if the moving company doesn't provide workers' compensation for their employees and contractors, it may be your responsibility to pay the medical bills for injuries suffered on your properties.

- Be prepared to read and understand the Bill of Lading – the contract between you and the movers laying out all the terms and conditions of the move. The mover must by law prepare a Bill of Lading for every shipment transported. The driver who will load your possessions must give you a copy of the Bill of Lading before loading your furniture and then after you're unloaded at the new house. Think of it as your receipt. Do not lose this important piece of paperwork, which is needed later to process a claim for missing or damaged items. Immediately, put it in your transition binder.

To Pack Yourself Or Not to Pack Yourself?

There are movers who will advertise that they will not only move you, but also pack your household goods, room by room, box by box. That is the reason that you are hiring them, right? Not so fast. You might be thinking, "Wait just a second. Did I need to do all that marking of furniture and packing myself?" The answer is YES -- if you want an organized move and strategic unpack in your new home.

Let's examine common practices. When deciding on a moving company, you meet with an estimator. Their job is to walk your property both inside and out to identify exactly what furniture and accessories you will be moving in order to estimate the actual cost. This process also allows them to estimate the packing materials needed, truck size and labor necessary to complete the move. The estimator's job is also to sell the other profitable services the company offers such as warehouse storage, crates for lighting fixtures and artwork. They will brag about their honors and awards, success in the industry and their wonderful referral base. Great.

You are typically assured of their ability to expertly handle your move without issue. You can really bond with a good estimator, and many clients do. They are often the "face" of the company and very good at their jobs, regardless of how they compiled their estimates, handwritten or electronic. Once the estimator is done compiling the estimate, you may never see him again. Typically, you will complete the process of signing paperwork and provide a deposit directly with the office.

This is an issue for you due to one very important reason. The estimator is not there on packing and/or moving day. You are starting all over. You will meet a totally new crew with a new crew leader. Hint: He will be the one who introduces the crew and holds the clipboard with the paperwork while assuming overall responsibility for the job. He will explain what they will do, you will nod and sign.

The leader is in charge of the project and will answer any questions you may have throughout the day. His level of expertise and communication skills are typically very good to excellent as he leads the crew. As the homeowner, the leader will be your source of communication.

If you choose to have them pack you, the crew will strategically scatter to begin the process. Brace yourself. They move very quickly to pack each room as carefully and speedily as possible. That's their job. You can attempt to oversee the process or even pack a box or two, but you can't be in every room at the same time. Crew members will be split into teams that either prepare and wrap furniture to load onto the truck or focus on packing boxes. They are there to move product and are not necessarily paying attention to the value of each fragile item. They don't know the difference or level of care to pack a glass floral vase from the local florist versus a Simon Pierce, Polish lead crystal or William Yeoward. They just pack it all while keeping up their rapid pace.

Their goal is to fill each box to the very top. It's typical for you to (someday and hopefully) find your fine china mixed up with your books, bric-a-brac and forks in one large box, a jumble of things that might still be whole…or in pieces.

As you recall, I've instructed you to pack by item type not by room, marking on the top and sides of the box itself exactly what is inside and where it goes by room in the new house. With larger items and furniture, you will specify on the blue tape its' final destination in the new house. Then you will add it to your inventory sheet. Meanwhile, John Q. Packer shows up and packs to fill that big box to the top and scribbles the contents on the top of the box. Or maybe not. He might just write the name of a room on top of the box and where it was packed, not necessarily the room these items belong in the new house. You will need to ask that the room be marked on *both* the top of the box and its sides so that when boxes are stacked the room name is still clearly visible.

The team leader will walk continuously throughout the house during this process placing colored, numbered stickers on each box and on your fine pieces of furniture that have been wrapped. The description is "chair" for a dining room chair, club chair, slipper chair, desk chair and leather chair. Perhaps you're already catching on when it comes to a major issue that's developing here. When they get to the new house and are unloading the furniture, they will stop to ask you where to put "the chair."

"Which chair?"

The movers who wrapped it have to peel back the furniture blanket because the guy with the inventory isn't around at the moment. He's inside the truck working on unloading. Meanwhile, you have no idea what the green numbered tag refers to or which room it should be placed in the new house until you see the actual chair. Ugh.

Remember when we touched each item in the old house and used the painter's tape and black Sharpies to decide which room this particular chair will go into when you arrive at the new house? Remember when I assured you that this would be a critical step for the move? Here's why: When the movers wrapped the chair at the old house, they placed your blue tape with the room designation ON TOP of the moving blanket. Bam! Problem solved. You know exactly where that chair goes and can direct them immediately. It's critical to walk continuously through the rooms to be sure that your furniture is wrapped correctly with your blue tape designation clearly displayed.

Even the most experienced packers and movers need to be reminded to watch the way they shrink wrap the skirt on the $7,000 custom sofa or fold $20,000 worth of drapery panels. This will save you a call to the designer to send someone to steam items back into their original shape. Extra attention also needs to be paid when packing large filigree mirrors to ensure that the decorative trim does not crack in transit if it's not being crated. Sweat these details. They matter. (If you don't know the specifics of how to do this properly then do an online search.)

A gentle reminder that hands should be washed and dried before attempting to wrap your white club chairs because handprints are a drag! Mattresses and box springs should also be marked with blue tape by room such as Master, Bedroom #1 and Bedroom #2. More about this later.

SMART MOVE: Confirm that each piece of furniture that leaves the house is clearly marked with your blue painter's tape and room designation for the new house. The tape should be placed in plain view with writing that is legible.

Since a moving inventory is not pictorial and movers aren't known for keeping an easily understood inventory, you'll never be certain if you have everything. You, your transition expert or move manager must be in charge of the day(s) and the quality of the pack and move process to ensure success.

Back to potential breakage of valuables and stains on fabric and furniture. I've seen movers pack expensive crystal with thin packing paper when I'd bubble wrap it after separating each piece (and the pieces of each piece). It's worth it to bubble wrap plates that cost $700 each or $50 if they have sentimental value. I've seen hundreds of broken items created by not using the correct packing materials. I have also personally witnessed a mover who accidentally cut his finger with an X-Acto knife and dripped blood on a beige custom sofa. Poor guy. Poor sofa. Movers move very quickly and get very sweaty -- it's expected. It only presents an issue when the sweat drips off their forehead onto your silk drapery panels that were just steamed in time to move to the new house. Disaster? No. Upsetting? Definitely. Breathe.

Enough said, except...take charge of your own move or have a transition expert and their crew pack your boxes by type, clearly identify the destination of each box on the top and sides, keep a detailed inventory and clearly tag wrapped furniture with its landing spot in the new house.

Fragile Items

Quite often I deal with gilt frames, fragile filigreed items and those couches with pleated skirts. Movers can be rough with these items because they're in the "get it out...get it in" mode. Don't be afraid to say: "That fragile lamp will need extra wrapping." Your movers should stop and listen to you.

Be sure that rugs are either folded or rolled carefully without creases. Rug pads should be shrink wrapped separately. Check that the ends of each rug are fully covered with paper and shrink wrapped to prevent soiling the edging. When they stand your beautiful rugs up and slide them into place on the filthy floor of the truck, you want to be sure the ends are not exposed. You will never be able to get this cleaned!

Logistics

Things Your Mover Won't Move:

- Aerosol Cans
- Ammunition
- Cleaning Products
- Fire Extinguishers
- Gasoline
- House Paints
- Open Alcohol Containers
- Open/Perishable Food
- Pets
- Plants
- Propane Tanks
- Welding Gas Tanks

It is critical to understand and follow correct procedures when moving into an apartment or condo building. It is your or your transition expert's responsibility to contact the building supervisor in advance of the move to reserve the loading dock and freight elevator. Check the specific hours you can begin and when the move must be completed. Your moving company will provide you with a Certificate of Insurance (COI) you will give to the building supervisor. In some cases, a popular moving company is already "known" to the building and the COI for that company is already on file. Additionally, it is common for a building to ask for a move deposit in case of damage caused by the move. This is typical and not negotiable. This fee also

The Top Items Damaged on Moving Day

- Drinking glasses
- Plates
- Artwork
- Lamp shades
- Wine and liquor bottles
- Mirrors
- Glass Pictures
- Books
- Stereo and audio equipment

According to Moving.Org

covers the cost to prepare for your move, pad the freight elevator and lay the hard, cardboard runners from the elevator to your unit to protect the floors.

Don't forget to ask if you need to secure parking permits for the movers and their smaller trucks and cargo vans. Once you have contracted with your moving company, call the new building to reserve your preferred move date. The first and last weeks of the month are popular move weeks. Don't delay the call if you have little flexibility with dates.

For house moves in cities and towns, be sure to order parking permits. These permits can be purchased online and must be clearly posted three days before the move date to prevent parking tickets and citations from being issued. You don't want to face a police order asking to remove your moving truck. I learned this lesson the hard way! I supervised a move years ago in a beautiful neighborhood in D.C. with wide, tree-lined streets and stately homes. We were loading two, 26-foot trucks and a cargo van. I failed to secure the moving permits for that neighborhood zone with the D.C. DMV and watched every two hours as the city employee in the little white car stopped to issue another ticket! At the end of the day, the crew leader handed me the tickets. While my clients did not care about the additional $300 they would pay in parking tickets, I did and never made that mistake again.

> **SMART MOVE:** Order city and town move parking permits and post three (3) full days before the actual move. Have twine and scissors ready to string the parking permits between signs or trees. They have two holes punched at the top of the permit for easy threading and placement along the twine, but they don't send you the twine or the scissors!

Final and Savvy Moving Tips:

- Never pay cash. You'll want a cashed check or credit card receipt as proof of the agreed upon services. We all have heard the horror stories of people who give cash deposits and then go to call their movers only to hear, "This number has been disconnected!" You don't want your movers to move themselves to the next town because they're scam artists.
- Don't ignore the condition of the moving truck. Ask to see the inside. Is it clean? Is there a company logo on the outside? Is the crew clean and professionally dressed?
- Check ProtectYourMove.gov and MovingScam.org to make sure your movers don't have a long history of "issues." If you're moving out of state then make sure your moving company has a U.S. DOT number, a unique license number issued by the U.S. Department of Transportation. You can make sure by checking their website. You can check your state's license database for local movers.

You've chosen a moving company and secured a move date. You have done your research, understand the fine print and are confident that you have made the best decision after carefully considering the options available to you. You sign the contract and provide a credit card deposit. You and the football are now at the ten-yard line and the goal is so close you can hear the crowd roar... touchdown!

It's time to prepare for the actual move.

Chapter Ten

Moving Day

Prepare for Moving Day

There are a million different things you'll need to track on moving day. It will be easier if you arrange for the following in advance to ensure that everything that you *can* control is *under* control before the truck pulls up:

- Arrange Internet and cable service ahead of the move at the new house, so you will be fully functional with ready access to update friends, family and keep track of your kids and pets. Avoid the need for service people to be in the new house on move day.

- Arrange with your security company to shutdown the system for your old house the day before the move. Make sure the security company will NOT appear at the new house until after the move as you won't have time to deal with their representative.

- Plan to arrange playdates for the kids and daycare for

the pets on moving day. To put it less kindly: Get rid of them! Ship them out! Doesn't really matter where -- grandma's, school, puppy class, or daycare, or have them hang out with friends. The last thing you need on move day is a bored child getting injured or a pet you need to keep your eye on. The chaos of moving day is emotionally upsetting to both.

- If you have trades working frantically to complete the punch list at the new house -- stop them. This is a day off for them and it's non-negotiable. Moving day is solely for you, your transition expert, and the movers. Make sure to confirm this with your contractor and crews ahead of time. If they show up anyway that day, do not give in. It's not a work day. Period.

- Use a design application to make a template of each room in the new house. Sketch in where you will put the major items (bed, couch, rugs, table, dresser). You'll use this as a road map on moving day and the days following the move when you are unable to think clearly and make a decision. You don't have to be a master artist. Just make a few key decisions about placement that can be changed at a later date. (My favorite moving apps are in the Appendix of this book.)

- Make a site visit. Take your blue painter's tape and black Sharpies with you to the new house before the movers arrive. If this is not possible due to time constraints or distance, you can do this while the movers prepare to unload the truck. Mark each room name on the blue tape and stick on the wall just outside the door. Remember that your mover will not know the difference between the media room, family room, den and library unless they are clearly marked.

- During this visit, use your template to create labels with the tape. Mark where the big furniture items will go on the tape (bookcases, beds, nightstands) by placing the tape on floors or on walls within the rooms.

- Leave your valuable jewelry stored in a safe deposit box, locked in the trunk of the car or with a neighbor for the day.

- Keep track of your purse, phone, keys (both new and old) and do not leave them unsupervised at any time. Don't forget your transition binder!

- Secure your financial documents, passports, birth certificates, social security cards and extra credit cards in a safe deposit box or in a locked safe for the day.

- Pack your car's front seat to include the "must-have" items that easily disappear during a move: phone chargers, computer cords, laptops, tablets, current family medication, inhalers, work bag, diaper bag, and checkbook.

- Prep the back of your car for one box that will contain "must-have" items for your first moments in the new house including a coffee maker, coffee, tea, a few mugs, sugar and creamer.

- Pack your tape measure and have it handy. You'll be glad you did when trying to straighten rugs and figure out furniture configurations.

- Pack cleaning supplies in your car for the new home

including heavy duty black contractor trash bags, 33-gallon regular-strength lawn and garden bags, paper towels, rags, sponges, and a good all-purpose cleaner for most surfaces like lemon-scented Fantastik. You can do one more swipe in cabinets and drawers before you put anything away. The trash bags are perfect to gather packing paper, bubble wrap, and other moving trash.

- Load boxes that will include items only **you** will hand carry and move like grandmother's priceless wedding crystal or valuable artwork. If it's extremely precious to you then you take it by car even if you have to make a few trips.

- Pack and bring a "go" bag for each member of the family (and pets) for the first few days in the house. This includes all keys, clothing for a few days, and toiletries.

- Set aside clean or new bedding for each bed that will be set up and slept in the first night (sheets, comforter, bed skirts, mattress pads, and pillows), so you can quickly set up the beds for the kids and yourself.

- Leave these things at the old house: architect plans, remotes, keys to all doors, and garage door openers.

- Plan to have a cleaning crew at your old house the day of the move or the next day to "broom sweep" the house after the movers leave. This is not a deep clean as you have done that recently, but you will want to clean the kitchen counters, refrigerator, freezer and oven if necessary, and make sure that all floors are vacuumed or swept. Bathrooms should be left in a pristine state. Leave your old home the way you hope someone will leave your new home. Remind the crew to remove all trash and cleaning supplies when they leave. Arrange to pick up and deliver the keys to your agent.

- Arrange to turn off everything at the old house including Internet, electricity, water, cable and gas. Gather cable boxes that must be physically returned or you'll face a steep fine.

- Go to the bank to withdraw several hundred dollars in fifties and twenties, so that you have it on hand at the end of the day to tip the movers. When you meet the crew in the morning at the start of the project, ask the team leader how many are in his crew for the day. Let him know that you intend to tip them out at the end of the day. If you mention this quietly to him in the morning, he will let his team know. This produces extra incentive to go above and beyond for you. A win-win.

Finally...It's Moving Day!

We might want to take away the exclamation point. Moving day is almost a letdown at this point in the process. It's exciting, but you're physically and emotionally exhausted and financially feel as if you have been used as actively as an ATM in the middle of a big city. You're not thinking clearly due to the prolonged upheaval of your lives, however, it's time to get your game face on. If you have a home transition expert, then it's his or her day to take charge, shine and shoulder the burdens of the day. If not, you have this book and transition binder close at hand.

There will be an early start to the day. You should be out of bed by six or seven a.m. to make sure you are getting started on the "last pack". This will include stripping all beds and bagging up the dirty sheets, shower towels and clothing. Do that last load of laundry in your old house, pack them clean and move them into the car. Pack all bathroom toiletries, shower soaps, gels and then head to the kitchen. Eat breakfast to provide strength for the day ahead.

What happens to your fridge contents during a move? During the "last pack," you will use boxes, bags and cold storage containers or coolers to pack the contents of your refrigerator and freezer. Yes, the movers can do this if you are not able, but you may want to pack your own food. This will give you one last opportunity to toss all those half empty bottles of condiments and last night's orange chicken – or better yet, plan ahead to get rid of as many items as possible on your last trash day in the old house.

Most movers show up at eight thirty or nine a.m. to start their day. If you have hired a transition expert to manage your day, you will not need to do anything, but say hello when introduced to the crew--if you are even there! Many of our clients actually opt out of this day entirely or will show up much later toward the end of the move.

SMART MOVE: Welcome the crew, identify the team leader (remember the clipboard!) and begin with a tour of the old house floor by floor. Explain that you will be available throughout the day to answer questions, address problems and direct furniture and box placement at the new house. Remind them that when the time comes you have your own inventory system that you will use to check off items as they come off the truck and into the front door.

You've already marked all the boxes on the top and sides with a black Sharpie marker where in big letters you've written: BEDROOM, KITCHEN, MASTER and BEDROOM #1. In spite of your diligence in clearly marking where you want boxes and furniture placed, expect there to be mistakes. It's not uncommon to find clearly marked boxes in the wrong rooms or furniture on the wrong walls. Know that it will happen – and it's okay. It will be fixed. At the end of the day, the final walk-through will allow you to direct these quick placement corrections before the crew leaves.

Wardrobe Boxes

Moving companies typically do not deliver wardrobes for your clothing until the day of the move. Why? Because they are bulky, unwieldy and take up a lot of floor space. That said, most of my clients don't like their clothing being touched by potentially dirty hands and risk having their beautiful and often expensive pieces jammed into wardrobes.

To avoid issues with the above, you should request delivery of the wardrobes several days ahead of the actual move date, so they can be packed in a proper order with clean hands. If you group like clothing together, unpacking in the new closets will be much easier, even if the closet configuration is a bit different.

This might seem like an extra step, but it will prevent other potential inconveniences like dry cleaning bills for incorrectly packed or soiled clothing.

Inventory

As we know, most movers will use a number, color and letter inventory system, which means nothing to you or me. What does green XYQ124 mean? Let's agree that this lettered and multi-colored system makes no sense to the average seller. How do you know when they put a tag on it that it will actually show up in the new location when they control the list that you can't even understand? I like to be in control of that list (as should you) to make sure that every single piece is checked off. While this step adds to the time it takes to load and unload a truck, it's crucial to maintain your own detailed inventory to easily track your furniture and boxes. Some savvy sellers even take pictures of certain precious, high-end or irreplaceable items in case they're damaged, so they can prove the condition that they were in before the move.

> **SMART MOVE:** A dated photograph is the kind of legal proof needed if a claim is challenged.

An experienced mover will also point out dings, scratches, loose furniture legs, and other issues during the packing and loading process. To provide our own clarity on this side of the move, my team adds a small piece of blue painter's tape on the damaged area to indicate that we acknowledge that the damage was present before the item was packed or moved.

SMART MOVE: Request careful placement of their numbered, color-coded stickers on furniture. Don't allow these stickers to be placed directly on antique wood, leather, suede, artwork, or gold-leaf frames and other delicate surfaces. When they are eventually removed, they may also remove the finish underneath or leave a permanent residue. Prevent damage and pay attention to where stickers are placed.

Loading the Moving Truck

The movers should start on your first floor by loading all packed boxes to create room to move and wrap furniture. They may take three or four boxes at a time and run up the truck ramp to fill what's known as "Grandma's Attic" or that area in the back of the truck just above the truck cab.

At the same time, another crew member should be wrapping the major furniture items including the sofa, dining room table, chairs, and other substantial pieces. The team leader should be compiling the moving company's inventory list. Remember to remind them to place your marked blue tape on top of the moving blanket and shrink wrap to easily identify the location of each piece in the new house.

Depending upon the size of your old home, the loading can take up to four to five hours. The goal is to have your old house loaded by one or one-thirty p.m. at the latest. You will want enough daylight hours to unload at the new place.

SMART MOVE: Purchase a case of water, Gatorade or soda and plan to provide lunch for the movers. It doesn't have to be fancy and can include pizza and sandwiches. Offer lunch options just after they arrive after completing the initial house tour. Inform them which bathroom to use throughout the day. Let the crew get right to work and keep humping until 12:30 p.m. when you will offer them lunch. This is a great way to intentionally limit the lunch period and avoid the movers going off property to find somewhere to eat. Plus, it spreads the good will with the moving team. A happy team is more productive and easier to work with. You will need this built-up goodwill later in the day for moving things again and again until they are just where YOU want them. While the movers are exhausted, and justifiably so, they are happy to comply.

Movers load rugs, mattresses, box springs and bed frames on the truck LAST so that they can remove them first as these pieces are the foundations for your rooms. It's a happy moment when they wheel down that truck door and say, "We're on the way to the new house."

You're eager to pull up to your new address.

Prep the New House and Start Unloading

Just like you did at your old house, you will give the crew leader a tour of the new house pointing out the room names in blue tape on the walls bedside the doors. Stop and allow the movers to prepare the new house with runners and necessary protection to avoid damage. Once they're done, they'll begin bringing in the rugs and bigger pieces of furniture while you check them off your own personal inventory list and guide the movers where to place them.

Be vocal during this process. For example, stand in your living room to announce, "Furniture on this side, artwork at the other end and boxes against this wall." Be specific. It's easy for the movers to leave a bunch of boxes marked "storage" in the laundry room, but it's equally easy (especially in your tired state) to forget that they're in there. I had a client who had 250 boxes being moved into a new kitchen. They wouldn't all fit in the new room, but I refused to let them spill into the hallway and block that pathway. You can find one empty room for extra boxes that you will unpack a few at a time.

Once all the furniture and boxes are off the truck and in the new house, start organizing the bedrooms. Stop and grab that bag of clean bedding in the car and put your bed together as if you were about to sleep in it now. Resist the urge to nap! Next stop: Set up the kids' beds.

It makes a new homeowner feel 1000 percent better when they know everyone has a freshly made bed to sleep in tonight. It won't be long before the movers have the other bedroom items in place including nightstands, dressers and lamps, which will make the room look complete. You will go to sleep tonight happy as a clam knowing that your bedroom is in decent shape.

Heavy Items

If you plan to move large safes, refrigerators, freezers, washers, dryers, total home gyms or other large and heavy items then make absolutely certain that you have marked the exact place in the room or area they will be installed using your blue painter's tape and black Sharpies. These items require tremendous manpower to move and you don't want them to be waiting while you decide where to place them – or worse yet – have them end up in the wrong room…or floor!

Televisions/Computers/Printers/Sound Systems/Speakers

Movers are happy to wrap your electronics and transport them. They will even remove TV brackets from the wall although they are not responsible for repairing the damage to the wall. They are also not responsible for installing the bracket in your new home or apartment. Plan for this, and if necessary, hire your AV and IT experts ahead of time to install your brackets and mount your televisions. They can also set up your stereo system and speakers if you do not have a built-in system in your new home.

With all of the stresses of moving, the last thing you need is to deal with difficult tech issues. It's money well spent to toss this job to the experts.

SMART MOVE: Save time and be present when the rugs are unwrapped and placed in each room to check that they are laid straight and placed exactly where you want them. Have a tape measure handy -- I do. It's better to do this before the furniture is placed or the mover will have to back up the furniture, move the rug and then move the furniture back into place. If you're someone who is a bit of a perfectionist (hello, I'm one) then make sure that the rug is straight to the inch. While I have an excellent eye, I am not shy about using my measuring tape to be sure. Ask the mover to move it a few times. You're paying a lot of money for their services and this is not out of line.

Communication on Moving Day

Don't get frustrated if there is a lack of communication with the workers. The critical connection for you is the team leader. It's tough when your main job on move day is to be sure that boxes and furniture are placed in the right rooms. You've prepared for this, yet you are still worn down by constant questions of where to put things all day long-- even though they are clearly marked. There are items that seem obvious, but are not marked such as gardening tools that are brought through the front door. Breathe. Inhale. Expect that boxes meant for the first floor will end up on the third floor. Basement storage ends up in the garage and sports equipment meant for the garage ends up in basement storage. It will happen. Exhale.

If you are losing control of the process and frustration is building, call for a quick meeting with the team leader. Explain your concern(s) and ask that nothing else be brought into the house until immediate changes are made. Don't compound the issue by continuing to unload.

Be clear about where you want boxes placed in each room. Pick a wall and stack them with the labeled contents facing out so that you can clearly see them. Do not fill the center of the room with boxes. Plan for kitchen boxes to be placed in the dining or family room, so that you can systematically unpack with enough room to lay out the contents. Tell them where to place the wardrobe boxes, so that they can be quickly unpacked directly into the closets and removed from the house.

Move Day Snafus – Expect Them

Over the thousands of moves I have coordinated and supervised, I am rarely surprised by - surprises. They happen with regularity, so be prepared to be surprised. Expect it. Be calm and ready to troubleshoot on the spot. One client's antique sofa had the legs and finials sawed off to fit through an outside door. How did they get it in there in the first place? At the old house, it was put into place before a renovation replaced the large sliding door with a smaller door.

Another client's sofa had to be hoisted out the master bedroom's French doors onto the lower roof and from there to the ground. We have also sawed a sofa in half to remove it from a basement. The sellers had offered to leave it and now everyone knew why. Be especially cognizant of furniture that was built on-site as you may have to completely disassemble or destroy the piece to remove it.

Downsizing to a smaller home? Be sure that your king or queen mattress will clear the turn on the stairs at the new place (although you won't know until the movers try it). A lot of people aren't aware that there is such a thing as a split box spring. While moving a couple from a 12,000-square foot house to a newly renovated luxury high rise, I was reminded of how things don't always fit. In order to ensure a smooth move, the estimator scheduled a site visit well before the actual move to scope out the loading dock, freight elevators, and back stairwell. This was necessary to accommodate large artwork, furniture, and sculptures. I thought they were prepared. I was wrong.

The move progressed without issue until the team leader pulled me aside to let me know that the 12-foot square glass dining room table top would not fit in the elevator or clear the turn on the back stairs to walk it up to the fourth floor. I went to the loading dock to see six movers holding the blanket wrapped table top. It was heavy and there were no options. The front desk agreed to store it until I could arrange for a crane to remove the outdoor railing on the balcony and hoist it through the French doors in the living room. In spite of my pleas, this crane company would not undertake this mission for several weeks due to rain, snow, and wind. Surprise? Definitely. But we handled it, and you will too, if you anticipate that issues will surely arise during a move. Don't stop the actual move but make time on the spot to discuss and resolve. Move on.

Cross-Country Moves

Cross-country moves differ in many ways as you add travel – for both you and your household goods – to the mix. You need to know that the way moving companies maximize profit is to make sure that the truck going from Illinois to Arizona or A to Z is completely full. If there is only a half full truck, then they lose the opportunity to make a profit on that shipment. This is why each truck often contains the entire lives of several families, which naturally leads to mixed up and lost items. I can't stress enough how important it is to keep your own detailed inventory lists for this type of move. Check it twice when that truck loads and unloads at your new home and be sure to report anything missing immediately. Things get lost like socks in a dryer.

You will want to consider the weather during a cross country move. The last thing you need is your moving truck getting stuck in some big mountain range during a snowstorm. One long distance move that I supervised from Washington, D.C. to Jackson Hole, Wyoming was complicated by the fact that we were moving the family's valuable wine cellar contents. The drivers of the moving truck had to drive straight through the night, so they didn't get caught in a rapidly approaching snowstorm and compromise the temperature of the wine. Be aware of the weather between Point A and Point Z and prepare for the inevitable delays that occur during the winter months.

A Quick Story: Bees and Honey

Years ago, I met a 53-foot moving truck for a family that was moving to D.C. from South Carolina. I knew that the decision to hire this company was based solely on cost because the client told me so. Maybe this company enjoyed a good reputation in their native state, but I found the men uncommunicative, slow and with negative attitudes. They were obviously tired and not happy to be there. The team leader sat on the back of the truck smoking cigarettes the entire day. Meanwhile, the men knew I was working on behalf of the new owners who were not present. When one of the movers put down one of the rugs in a crooked manner, I asked him to straighten it.

"Look lady," sniped the mover. "We're not decorators. We're *just* movers."

I refused to lose my temper and said, "After we straighten the rug, we'll need to move the boxes marked family room out of the living room. They're still in the living room. Thank you."

I had no recourse with these movers, as I hadn't hired them and wouldn't be able to hire them again since we didn't live in the same state. But I was still respectful and kind. What would losing my temper accomplish? They would have just been less cooperative, and they were pretty rude in the first place. Getting in a tiff with them so early in the morning would have made it worse for the entire day.

I've always believed that you get more bees with honey. **SMART MOVE**: I brought out a plate of chocolate chip cookies and cold Gatorade at three p.m. when the men were really lagging. The next few hours went smoothly, and they did everything I wanted because they really appreciated that small extra effort. 'Nuf said.

It's Almost Over

It won't be long before it's dark outside and the movers are unloading the last of your household goods. How will you know? You'll see some of the crew folding those heavy moving blankets and putting them back in the truck followed by the march of the empty wardrobe boxes. You can ask them to take your recently empty unpacked boxes and packing material while they have room on the truck. Remember the goodwill I mentioned this morning? The movers don't have to take them, but many are happy to do so after the drinks and lunch you offered. You can help by quickly dragging any empty boxes into hallways for them to remove.

Final Walk-Through

The last thing you will do before signing the final Bill of Lading is to ask the team leader to do a final walk-through with you. You will check each room carefully to be sure each contains what it should... and the heavier pieces of furniture and rugs are in the right place.

Once the final walk-through is completed, your team leader will call the office to close out your invoice. Make sure that he compiles a list of any unused packing material purchased from the company for the move and indicates this on the Bill of Lading. This return should reflect a credit along with the deposit you paid to reserve the move. He will inform you of the balance due and the movers will want to be paid that day. You will sign off on the Bill of Lading, confirm method of payment for the balance due and receive copies of this document for your records. Keep them readily accessible in your transition binder. You may need them.

If something was damaged during the move process, you will already have documented this and made the team leader aware. I will clearly mark on the Bill of Lading that damages are still pending. As for the rest of the household goods, you will not sign off on damages as it's late and you can't possibly be expected to check each item right now. Over the next few days, you can carefully document any damages including taking photos of each item. Be sure to ask exactly who you will contact in case of damaged or missing items. Make sure you have a copy of the mover's inventory list, so it will be easy to cross reference the damaged items at a later date and process a claim.

Tip the Movers?

The answer is YES if they have done everything possible to accommodate your requests and have made a long, difficult day easier for you. You have cash on hand and will give them each an amount that reflects your gratitude for a job well done. My rule is to give each member of the moving crew $50 a day and the crew leader double, which is $100. If the move takes more than one day, then you will tip them out at the end of *each* day because you don't know if you will have the same crew the following day.

It's common for the team leader to return the following day, but the crew may be different. Moving companies do try to keep the crew together for the duration of the move, but it is not always possible.

You're Home. Finally.

The good news is if you're staying in the house tonight you have a warm, clean bed waiting for you. Don't try to unpack *at all* the night of your move because you're exhausted. Take a long, hot shower, order some dinner and then fall into your old bed in your new digs. You did it! You're almost there!

Chapter Eleven

Get Settled: It's Finally About You

The next morning, it will feel downright odd. Where are you? Oh yes, you've moved. You're home.

You're waking up at your new home in your old bed, but nothing else is the same because your entire life is still in boxes. The roller coaster runs screaming down the next loop and so do you. You are overwhelmed -- again! There is still so much to do. Back to the emotional (you have nothing left to give), financial (how much more do I have to spend on this move) and physical (hard labor) mix. There hasn't been time to plant any emotional ivy.

You've come this far.

You will make it to the end of the ride.

The first task at hand is to strategically unpack rooms in order of importance. If you had your mover unpack the day before then everything is on the floor in each room, which is typically unorganized and truly disturbing. If you are working with a transition expert, they are hard at work carefully unpacking each room with an eye towards organizing every drawer, nook and cranny. Or perhaps you're going it alone. Maybe you're on kitchen duty while your husband, partner, mother or friend unpacks the bathrooms and the kids take care of their own bedrooms.

Split up the labor force to focus on the children's bedrooms and bathrooms first because the kids are chomping at the bit to settle their spaces and start their new lives. Kids will need a place to unwind and play while those tender new emotional ivy plants begin to root as they get used to the new house. Another group will focus on the master bedroom although you can hold off on final organization of the master closets for now.

Your next focus will be to unpack and settle the family room or great room to provide a place to flop on a familiar couch and watch a movie to celebrate your move into the new home. Later.

A transition expert will make sure that you're working on the right rooms and in the right order rather than unpacking several rooms at the same time and just spinning your wheels.

There is a strategic way to approach unpacking. The good news is unpacking is a lot easier than packing despite the fact that there are 450 boxes around the house and your clothes (fresh out of the wardrobe box) look like a mess in your new closet. For the best results, I recommend unpacking rooms in the following order of importance:

- Kids' bedrooms and baths
- Master bedroom and bath
- Great room

Don't forget, you still have more things. If you have items located in off-site storage the time is now (or in the next few days) to transfer what you'll want to the new house.

Remember Your Template

Earlier, I asked you to create a template of all the rooms in your new house and where you want the furniture to be placed. This will prove invaluable today, the day after your physical move, because you won't want to think. You'll just want to *do.*

Stick to the template as you begin to unpack knowing you can always switch things around later. Of course, be ready for surprises. You've planned the layout and every piece fit perfectly on "paper," but in reality, it may be tighter than you thought. It just doesn't look or feel right. Be prepared to move things around as the design you've created is not set in stone. Be open to seeing and using your furniture in new and interesting ways. Sound familiar? That walnut table that used to be in your living room in the old house really does look perfect in the new great room. Shake things up and move it there.

This is, after all, a new chapter. A makeover is in order.

> **SMART MOVE:** Purchase new hangers for the closets. Felt hangers, which come in a variety of colors although you will just choose one color, are an excellent choice for bedroom closets that are space saving and attractive. Solid wooden hangers are perfect for the front foyer closet.

Kitchen. Open all kitchen boxes. Unwrap and lay contents on counters, table and floor to view all that you own and see it in one glance. What items should be close to the stove? What kitchen tools are your must-have items? As you put the items away, do so in a way that's organized with a focus on how your new kitchen was designed to function. This will make the decisions easier for you and the end result will be a perfectly organized and functional space. One of the first areas I set up is the coffee/tea station and the breakfast bar for the kids who need easy access to cereal, bowls, and silverware.

Pantry. Organize by types of foods and liquids. All drinks are together on a lower shelf for easy access. What you use the most should be eye-level including canned goods, pastas and rice. Remember to line up all soups together while beans are next to beans. Keep seldom used items like party bowls and platters, extra glasses, fancy napkins and entertaining pieces on higher shelves to keep them out of the way. If there are a lot of loose packet items, invest in small baskets to store them neatly and in plain view to locate quickly. Keep snacks for younger kids at a lower level in plastic containers for easy after school munchies.

Laundry room. Moving is a dirty business, so you must settle this room quickly as you will need it. This room should be organized by area: laundry, cleaning supplies, and overflow pantry items. If you stick with this method of grouping "like" items, you will always know when it's time to restock.

Living and dining room. Use the dining room to continue to store all artwork until you have the room to unpack. Line up items along the walls to view and choose which pieces will be hung in each room or area.

> **SMART MOVE:** Slow down and take your time to think about the placement of each item. There aren't any hard deadlines now, except your own. Don't expect to be totally unpacked and settled in one day. This is unrealistic if you want to be organized and mindful about the decisions you are making.

Attic, garage and storage spaces. These areas can wait until you have the mental and physical strength to tackle them. Think big picture and be sure that you have the correct size and style containers to organize the items you will store in each area. Ask yourself: Where will I store the mementos we each saved? Do the holiday ornaments go in a big closet in the basement or in plastic boxes up to the attic? Home Depot offers many different styles and sizes of hard plastic bins for storage, even some with holiday colored tops: red for Christmas, orange for Halloween, and so on. Set up a gift gallery with a wrapping station in an extra closet or an empty bedroom with built-in cabinets. This will make last minute gift giving a breeze as you will organize the gifts by type: hostess, family, boy birthday, girl birthday, and holiday.

Proper shelving units are a must for Type A homeowners. They provide visual organization and physical storage in your new location and you may need them in different sizes and styles for different rooms. Consider shelving to organize basements, attics, garages, caged storage in apartment buildings and laundry rooms. Another personal "go to" are the metal shelves in varying heights and widths available at Home Depot in wire, chrome or steel. While hard plastic or wood might be less expensive, temperature differentials and heavy weight will affect them over time. Make sure that you take proper measurements of space including height, width and depth when it comes to shelving units. They're heavy to carry and take time to assemble. You don't want to make careless mistakes and find yourself racing back to the store.

No mudroom? Create a cubby area. Perhaps this is in the laundry room or even in the garage. You can invest in a cubby system that needs minimal assembly, but works wonders in a house full of kids. My personal favorite is the Kallax shelving system with decorative baskets from IKEA. A Home Depot white hook board with multiple large hooks hung above the Kallax shelf will keep everything organized. Kids can keep their shoes, backpacks and sports bags in one place. You can use it for grocery bags, dog leashes and keys to the cars and house. Train your family to use the new cubby area instead of leaving things by the front door or on the kitchen table or counters. Create a cubby spot and you'll never regret it.

Getting settled in your new home takes time and should be done with the intention of planting your emotional ivy throughout each room and area of the home. This time it is about YOU, your family and making this new house a home. Unpacking your boxes allows you to touch each of the items you decided was important enough to make the move, so enjoy the process of placing them lovingly where you want them to go.

SMART MOVE Details:

Be organized! Set aside time to think about installing built-ins and bookshelves that will display the books, decorative objects, photos and mementos you have chosen for this room.

Be adventurous! Perhaps you have decorative items that don't have "a home in your new home." Keep them in your staging area or the dining room, perhaps on the table, in order to see what is available. Have fun displaying your treasures in different rooms. Just because that vase was in the dining room of the last house doesn't mean it wouldn't be perfect in your new bedroom. Who doesn't like to wake up to fresh flowers from the outside garden?

Be well-rested! Don't expect to be ultra creative when you are physically and emotionally tired. The quality of your decisions will be poor, and you will make mistakes. Wait a few days until you feel more like yourself to put your personal stamp on the house.

Be generous! Donate items that do not fit into the new design scheme rather than placing them in the attic or storage room. The only comment I ever hear is: I wish I would have gotten rid of it earlier or why did I pay to move this thing in the first place?

Be patient! Accept and embrace the reality that your new home is a work in progress. It's okay to allow yourself time to breathe while you figure this all out.

Boxes and Packing Materials

There is nothing more satisfying than emptying a box and knowing that all the items are placed exactly where you want them to be. You will be eager to remove the empty boxes, packing paper, art paper and bubble wrap from your home as quickly as possible. Put them out with your recyclables or the night before the scheduled pick up, so that neighbors who may be moving can snag them off the street. Note: All moving companies charge to return to remove your used empty boxes and packing materials. This service is not free or included as part of your move.

Don't be tempted to leave "just a few boxes" in certain rooms. Unpack all boxes even if you are not ready to work in that room. It will look and feel more settled and reduce the emotional stress of seeing stacked boxes. Pick one room to house the items that you are not sure where to place. We have discussed the dining room to serve this function for the moment to allow you time to make decisions.

Are you done yet?

Almost! That roller coaster is pulling into the station for the last time.

Chapter Twelve

Transitioned

Congratulations! By now, your old house is a new home to others and your new house is slowly beginning to feel like home. There is still a lot to be done while new routines are established, and you settle into your new space and new life. You have FINALLY unstrapped the safety harness and stepped off the roller coaster ride for the last time! Yes, the journey was long, arduous and expensive. But you did it. **You decided to move, made choices based on TRUTH and accurate, up-to-date information, partnered with me and trusted the value of the expertise provided in this guide.**

Sure, there were unwelcome surprises, bumps and bruises along the way. Anyone who has ever moved their home and changed their life has a story to tell. You're sure to have one, too. The home transition is almost over. It's time to plant the emotional ivy that will make this new house, HOME.

Rome Wasn't Built In A Day

With each passing day, you will feel more settled, but Rome wasn't built in... a day. It will take time to create the home that you envision and are determined to create. The initial unpacking might take up to five to seven days to truly be complete. There is no timeline for this part of the process except the timeline you set for yourself. Proceed slowly and methodically to make meaningful, well- thought-out decisions that will affect your space and how you use it as time passes and you continue to settle in.

It's now time to invite family, friends and neighbors to come by and help welcome you to the new home. Reach for the platters you packed months ago that seem like "new" to you now and use them to serve your guests. Enjoy this "work in progress" and allow the tempo of your new life to unfold in a timeframe that is realistic and manageable for you and your family.

Be honest and firm but gentle with yourself during this settlement period. There will be furniture and other items that you insisted needed to be packed and moved that you now realize don't actually fit into the overall design scheme and function of the house -- donate them. Not ready yet? Then store them for a definitive period of time and choose to delay the decision for now. This reevaluation happens with each and every move. For example: Mom's Oriental rug is just too dark for the new dining room. You swore it would look great, but in reality, it looks terrible and overwhelms the room. Still not ready to let it go? Store it for a specific amount of time and if you still cannot think of how to use it -- donate it!

The Total Home Transition^{SM} process is a marathon, not a race. A gentle reminder dear Reader, it took us a week, or two, or even three to purge things during the initial organizing, sorting and packing phase. It will take time to create well-designed rooms that reflect your personal taste in the new home. Slow down. It's worth it to take your time because you will be happier with the outcome. Why rush?

SMART MOVE: Stop. Breathe. Emotionally regroup and rebalance. Physically rest and repair. Financially review and reconcile. You're home.

After a few weeks of living in your new home, you'll begin to understand the space and how your family functions within it. Maybe the great room is barely used because everyone is really enjoying that lower level family room. For now. It may change over time. Perhaps the kitchen counter has become "the eating spot" in the house instead of the kitchen table. Be open to surprises. Adapt.

Watch closely how your family is actually using the new space. One family who never used the lower level family room in their old house can't tear themselves away from the new "movie theater" downstairs in the new home. A third-floor loft area has suddenly become Dad's favorite work space instead of his formal library. Just allow yourself to live and be open to change and new decisions that need to be made. For instance, in the new home a family insisted that the front of the fridge remain clutter-free. The only problem was they kept the daily calendar there and now no one knew what was going on. Chaos ensued. What ultimately worked was a bulletin board in the adjacent laundry room with a calendar, space for permission slips, art work, and other fun things like coupons to that new pizza place. Problem solved.

There is always a solution, but sometimes you need actual time to figure it out in unfamiliar situations and spaces. Another family had a large storage room (an old laundry room) downstairs that was empty. We turned it into a craft room with new chrome shelving to hold all the arts and crafts supplies. This delighted the kids and Mom who encouraged the use of the old laundry sink for quick clean-ups. The challenge is to identify your family's needs and to discover and create the space to accommodate them.

Your move is still a work in progress, but you've hit the sweet spot where you're in the new home and exploring new possibilities. Wise words for your peace of mind: A Total Home Transition^{SM} can take up to a year to be fully complete.

Reconciliation

The financial reconciliation will need to be done to get a truly accurate accounting of exactly how much this moving process cost from house to house. This is a truly sobering moment for many sellers. In spite of the informed and educated choices you made, you now realize just how wrong you were with the overall "budget" you set aside in your mind. As was described earlier in this book, moving is expensive.

Make sure to process claims with your moving company quickly as many movers have a time limit within which you must file a claim for it to be processed. Back to the binder.

New homeowners often find themselves with unexpected home improvements and the need for repairs they did not anticipate. Expect this and understand that it is not uncommon. Address and repair issues as they arise in order of importance and stay calm. Take advantage of insurance policies to fix what your home inspector might have missed.

One of the closing steps in the home transition journey is the phone call or visit to your tax accountant. It's time to gather all the carefully filed paperwork and receipts in the binder that relate to the sale of the previous house and move to inquire about the financial implications and deductions you are entitled to utilize. You will now be introduced to and become intimately familiar with the IRS 523 form and its application in the sale of a primary residence. You will wish you weren't.

Getting Settled

One day in the not too distant future, you'll be sitting in your new home, sipping your coffee, and you'll feel it. You're actually a bit out of sorts, and even bored, yet you can't put your finger on what's wrong. It's typical after a long home transition process to feel a physical and emotional letdown after it's finally over. From the moment you decided to move, through the prep and sale of your house and the ultimate move to your new home, you have been busy managing exactly how to get from where you started (there) to where you are (here). The pace was frenetic and your mind remained on constant overload as you focused on the thousands of decisions you had to make. You were operating on survival mode for a long period of time.

So why are you feeling a bit… lost and let down?

It's normal to think that this strange feeling you have is "odd" or "wrong". You have reached the ultimate destination and everything that you organized and planned for is now completed. You should be happy, right? Remember, the roller coaster has pulled back into the station and the ride is over, but your legs may still feel unsteady. The adrenaline rushes you counted on to carry you through the "ride" is gone. This too shall pass. So, will the visceral memory of the emotional, financial and physical "pain" you experienced along the way. You will begin to reimagine the journey as thrilling and exciting at certain points and long and difficult in others. You might now think, "Wait, that wasn't so bad." (That's what I promised you in the beginning!) But THIS observation is made with hindsight and without emotion. You are truly settling into your new home.

Change is hard, and you'll need time to adjust. You had the courage and determination to make difficult but meaningful choices based on TRUTH that saved you time, money and endless aggravation. You were focused and effective during this major transition. Take a moment to savor the journey and congratulate yourself for surviving one of life's biggest stressors. You followed my Total Home Transition[SM] process and your emotional, financial and physical world is back in balance.

Smile! Let your ivy take root and bring you happiness.

Welcome home.

THE END

Afterword

Thank you for reading my first book. Please join me for further home transition advice, tips and stories at www.CarolineCarter.com.

Appendix

    This Appendix is meant to spark your imagination to update your house to appeal to a wide variety of qualified buyers. These choices in no way represent all the options available in stores and online that address different styles, finishes and price points. Consider this a handy resource list that may change with the prevalent styles of the day and with what's appropriate or current in your town, city and region of the country. I've focused on the rooms that are updated the most, especially kitchens and baths. I've also included my go-to neutral choices for paint, lighting and flooring throughout the home.

    A quick disclaimer: The houses I have worked on represent just a microcosm of the size, style and price points across the country. In no way do I expect that these choices will be the only options or necessary for every seller to consider.

Resources

REALTORS

- National Association of REALTORS®
  https://bit.ly/2MmsUbu

MOVING AND STORAGE INFORMATION

- American Moving and Storage Association (AMSA)
  https://www.moving.org/

- Move.org
  https://www.move.org/
  This site helps you find, compare and hire professional movers. It is a great source of information for both local and long distance moves and provides tips, tools and advice. A must read for sellers.

MOVING APPS

- Unpakt
  https://www.unpakt.com
  Free
  Find a moving company by entering the basics about when, where and what you're moving.
  Available in the App Store for iPhone, iPads and in the Google Play Store for Androids.

- Sortly
  https://www.sortly.com/
  Free Trial with Purchase Plan
  Compartmentalize every inch of your house and create a moving checklist, photograph items and categorize them by location.
  Available on the App Store and the Google Play Store.

- MakeSpace
  https://makespace.com/
  Free
  Downsizing or moving to a home with less storage space? Book an appointment for movers to pick up your household goods and deliver it to storage.
  Found on the App Store or on Google Play Store.

- Dolly
  https://dolly.com/
  Free
  Find vetted and insured pick-up truck owners to help with your move, furniture pick-up and hauling away what you no longer need and want. Dolly provides extra muscle at your home to move things around.
  Found on the App Store and the Google Play Store.

- Flying Ruler
  http://www.flying-ruler.com/
  $1.99
  Acts as your tape measure, ruler, protractor and angle-measurer to make sure your new sofa will fit in your living room. You calibrate on your phone.
  Found on the App Store and Google Play Store.

HOME INSPECTORS

- American Society of Home Inspectors
  WWW.ASHI.ORG/FIND

APPRAISERS

- American Society of Appraisers
  http://www.appraisers.org/Home

JUNK/FURNITURE/WASTE REMOVAL

- College Hunks Hauling Junk and Moving
  http://collegehunkshaulingjunk.com

- 123 Junk
  https://www.123junk.com/

- Chemicals, Paints, Other Solid Waste Products
  www.epa.gov
  Check your state's rules and regulations for disposing of chemicals, toxins and paint.

DONATIONS

- Charity Choices
  www.CharityChoices.com

ESSENTIALS

- Scotch Blue Painter's Tape-.94x60
  https://thd.co/2DqPigY

- ▢ Black Sharpies
  https://thd.co/2R4r27N

- ▢ GE Soft White Light Bulbs (60, 100, 50-100-150 watts)
  https://bit.ly/2U24eHG

EXTERIOR

- ▢ Shutters
  https://thd.co/2MneK9Y

- ▢ Lighting

  Sea Gull Light Fixture
  https://thd.co/2DqkA7L

- ▢ Black Rustoleum Spray Paint
  https://thd.co/2AZ7Y5I

- ▢ Wire Brush
  https://thd.co/2CCrjto

- ▢ House Numbers

  Baldwin -4.75 " House Numbers
  https://bit.ly/2W3ua7T

- ▢ Door Handsets

  Schlage –Plymouth
  https://thd.co/2FRb3YT

Kwikset-Arlington
https://thd.co/2DrQKzP

- Door Knocker

    Baldwin-Ring Knocker
    https://thd.co/2T6kHdX

    Baldwin –"S" Knocker
    https://thd.co/2U7qQXs

- Kickplate

    Schlage Bright Brass Kickplate
    https://thd.co/2sHRF8N

- Mail Slot
    https://thd.co/2TdKm4k

- Welcome Mats

    Coir Rectangle
    https://thd.co/2RCHQI8

    Shell Mat-Coir
    https://thd.co/2U2RDEp

- Urns
    https://thd.co/2sCaKJN

INTERIOR

- **PAINT**
  Benjamin Moore
  Navajo White
  Classic Gray
  White Dove
  Simply White
  Ceiling White
  www.benjaminmoore.com

- **FLOORING**
  Ceramic Tile
  https://thd.co/2AScvqv

  Vinyl Tile
  https://thd.co/2tqpnmM

  Black Granite Tile
  https://thd.co/2Qbqbqr

  Home Decorators Collection Engineered Hardwood
  Flooring (Gray)
  https://thd.co/2R5bXTs

- Polish/Cleaner
  Quick Shine Multi Surface Floor Finish and Polish
  https://thd.co/2sCbC11

- Rejuvenate Wood Floor Professional Restorer –Satin
  https://thd.co/2FP5kTt

- ❏ Carpeting

    Mohawk Flooring/Sisal-Impressions-Raffia
    https://bit.ly/2Dq5yi9

- ❏ Area Rugs

    Home Depot Seagrass 8x10
    https://thd.co/2DruPbT

LIGHTING

- ❏ Bedroom
    https://thd.co/2F4Yndn

- ❏ Dining Room
    Home Decorators Collection 6-Light Crystal Chandelier
    https://thd.co/2WbtkGj

    Hampton Bay 6-Light Crystal Chandelier
    https://thd.co/2FF6T74

- ❏ Lower Level Family Room
    4-Light White Electric Cloud
    https://thd.co/2sxIl7w

KITCHEN

- ❏ Drawer Pulls
    https://thd.co/2R11oRy

- Cabinet Door Knobs
  https://thd.co/2Odt447

- Dining Table
  Ballard Designs- Essential Skirted Side Table (29.5 x 48")
  https://bit.ly/2RFPCRU

BATHROOMS

- Wall and Floor Tile

  Carrara Marble
  https://thd.co/2W8ROQk

  White Ceramic
  https://thd.co/2T4Ita9

  Cream Ceramic
  https://thd.co/2uK74ar

- Vanities with Tops: Various sizes and colors

  Home Decorators Collection
  https://thd.co/2T6fmDz

  Glacier Bay
  https://thd.co/2FFGshS

- Kohler Sink-Memoirs
  https://thd.co/2U7y6m2

- Kohler Toilet-Memoirs
  https://thd.co/2GBc9Gn

- Faucets: 4" and 8" spread in a variety of finishes

  Kohler-Forte
  https://thd.co/2sxNlci

  Kohler-Devonshire
  https://thd.co/2RCXByS

  Moen-Banbury
  https://thd.co/2MmBA1y

  Delta-Silverton
  https://thd.co/2FN5vPb

- Lighting: Sold in 2 and 3 Light, various finishes

  Hampton Bay
  https://thd.co/2u8TVqg

  Sea Gull
  https://thd.co/2MlsNNr

- Medicine Cabinet: Surface Mount

  Kohler-Mirrored
  https://thd.co/2FMVLEq

  Home Decorators Collection: Surface Mount White
  https://thd.co/2FFc9aO

◻ Hardware Sets: Sold in various sizes and finishes

Kohler-Forte
https://thd.co/2Wb9bAa

Kohler-Devonshire
https://thd.co/2FGinra

Moen -Banbury
https://thd.co/2sD0GjB

Delta -Greenwich
https://thd.co/2sxTSnm

Delta-Silverton
https://thd.co/2yzqks9

◻ Shower Curtain Rod

Tension
https://thd.co/2T1WRA5

Installed Straight
https://thd.co/2TdPAwY

Installed Curved
https://thd.co/2RHfgFT

DÉCOR

The following items can be found at: HomeGoods, TJ Maxx, Marshalls and Target:

- White bath and hand towels
- Matelassé shower curtain-white–72" x 72"
- Shower curtain liner-white or clear–72" x 72"
- Shower curtain rings-brushed nickel or chrome
- Tissue holder
- Trash can
- Crystal or ceramic white soap dish or soap dispenser
- Guest soaps in white or cream

BEDROOMS

- Plantation Window Blinds
  Faux Wood Blind (1 inch)
  https://thd.co/2W92pLd

- Plantation Window Shutters
  Traditional Faux Wood White Interior Shutter
  https://thd.co/2T6Avxs

- Air Mattress
  Intex Comfort Plush Elevated Dura-Beam Airbed, Queen
  https://amzn.to/2W395dF

- Bed Pillows

  The Big One (standard and king)
  https://bit.ly/2FFXQmq

- Bed skirt-All Sizes

  Made By Design-Solid Bed Skirt (white)
  https://bit.ly/2HsrTzJ

- Matelassé coverlet in twin, full/queen and king (white or cream)

- Matelassé shams in standard, king and euro (white or cream)

MUDROOM/LAUNDRY ROOM

- Utility Sink
  https://thd.co/2AVzYto

- Laundry Cabinet/Sink Combo
  https://thd.co/2FPlV9C

- Ikea Kallax Shelving Unit
  Note: Turn on side and hang the hook rack over the top of it
  https://bit.ly/2MruS9m

- Hook Rack 24" Wood White Board with 5 Brushed Nickel Hooks
  https://thd.co/2ATkB2t

- Boot Tray
  https://thd.co/2DVOG3L

STORAGE/GARAGE

- HDX -Chrome Shelves
  https://thd.co/2RYyd6g
  https://thd.co/2FQ1ZDE

SCENTS

- Candles

  Nest: Holiday Classic Candle (November and December)
  https://bit.ly/2FNh74u

  Nest: Lemongrass & Ginger (all year)
  https://bit.ly/2FNe0Kd

- Odor Neutralizing Gel Beads

  Up & Up Fresh Linen Scented Gel Beads
  https://amzn.to/2SXJ6Ch

  Smells Begone Fresh Cotton Odor Neutralizing Gel Beads
  https://amzn.to/2FO1gmD

- Room Sprays

  Lysol Lemon Breeze Indoor Spray
  https://bit.ly/2MhjH45

  Lysol Spray Crisp Linen
  https://bit.ly/2MjiA3Y

  Febreze Linen and Sky
  https://bit.ly/2RTQWje

CLEANING PRODUCTS

These products are sold at Home Depot and most grocery stores:

- Lemon Fantastik
- Bounty paper towels
- Brillo Pads
- CLR for Calcium, Lime and Rust
- Mr. Clean Magic Erasers
- Clorox with Bleach-Lemon Scent
- Lemon Pledge
- 5x Resolve
- Windex
- Easy-Off Fume Free
- Comet
- Bar Keepers Friend Soft Cleanser
- Soft Scrub
- Lysol Clean and Fresh
- Mr. Clean-Lemon Scent
- Scrubbing Bubbles Bathroom Cleaner
- Quick Shine Multi Surface Floor Finish and Polish
- Rejuvenate Wood Floor Professional Restorer -Satin Finish
- OxiClean Pet Fresh Carpet Powder

Acknowledgements

As a huge reader, I always read the book in its entirety including the acknowledgements page. I do this as a way to slowly detach from the book, but also because I am curious about who the author thanks and why. I'm often impressed with the author's detailed recall to thank pages of people who helped them to bring the book to fruition, but never understood how they could remember the entire list. Now, I do. It takes a great many people to create a book. It took a great many people to create *this* book.

Writing this book as a new author was a huge challenge for me. I am more comfortable having a conversation with someone. So, I did. My editor, Cindy Pearlman of Big Picture News, Inc., allowed me to talk, and talk and talk about a topic that I am passionate about and helped me to put the hours of our conversation into a format that makes sense for you to read. Thank you, Cindy! You are a superstar at what you do!

To those early "believers" in Done In A Day, I am grateful for your support: Michael Seay, Vice President, Long & Foster; Michael Rankin, Managing Partner, TTR/Sotheby's International Realty; Dana Landry, Founding Partner and Principal Broker, Washington Fine Properties and the hundreds of real estate agents and clients you have recommended our services to over the last 14 years.

To the thousands of clients I have worked with who took a professional and personal interest in my business and my career: April Delaney, Anita McBride, Laura Cox Kaplan, Preben Ostberg and Stuart

Bloch, it made a difference to me that you cared enough to share your insight and expertise. I wish I could mention each and every client I have learned from over the years, the list is endless.

To the Done In A Day "Girls", as you are known throughout the Washington, D.C. area, you are and have always been the "glue" that keeps this company together. The original team of: Magie Maling, Elena DeLeon, Alberto ("Betcha") Lamagna, Rodeliza (Liza) Lamagna, Luz Funeles, Racquel Torres, Elsa Tutor and the many other design assistants who have been part of our teams through the years -- I thank you. Truly.

To Al Florez, Steve Kahn and Ali Rostami, you have become family since 2005, and this book could not have been written without your dedicated guidance in providing valuable information for our clients about the worlds of: painting, contracting, electrical, carpeting and rugs, among other things.

To Eric Turner, hauler extraordinaire and right hand, who never questioned or complained. Your loyalty and reliability has always been appreciated.

To Herbert Sanchez, landscape genius whose teams helped to create gardens to sell for our clients. Each property is a new adventure with you.

For the early readers; Rida D'Agostino and Lisa Ireton, your collective input made this a better book and your confidence in the message and constant support kept me off the "ledge".

To Karen Kelliher, editor extraordinaire, this book is leaps and bounds more perfect than I ever dreamed it could be because of you.

To Sherri Cunningham of CP Communications who made sure that the Readers knew exactly where to find me -- thank you.

To Linda Caldwell and Emily Tippetts at Tippetts Book Design, you created a book cover I am proud to call my first.

To Tony Powell, photographer to the stars, I am in awe of your extraordinary vision and talent and humbled that you made time to photograph ME.

To Mary Richardson, best friend and original mentor, who taught me in the early years about the importance of my "buckets," the chart of accounts on the P & L and how to work poolside -- so that we could tan and work at the same time --genius.

To Bill O'Neill for his wise counsel and legal opinion when I needed it -- and I needed it. There is no adequate way to thank you except to say, thank you.

To Christina Carter, steadfast support my entire life -- I am truly blessed to call you, sister.

To Buddy Carter, for the thousands of hours we spent through the years discussing the real estate industry, its challenges, changes and the financial impact to the seller. I could not have written this book without your insight, guidance and belief that the message was important enough to share and that I was the one who needed to share it.

To Philip Carter, whose support was welcomed and appreciated each time I needed it. Thank you, brother.

To Mary Carter and Howard Carter, it's an honor to be your daughter. You never doubted me for a minute!

The personal and professional journey of the last 14 years has been made for one reason only -- my three beautiful children: Cecilia, Grace and Harrison Carter. You are and will always be at the center of my life and the reason I get up each morning with a smile on my face.

CPSIA information can be obtained
at www.ICGtesting.com
Printed in the USA
LVHW050202060719
623119LV00015BA/574/P

9 781733 696111